We Live in the Alaskan Bush

We live in the
ALASKAN BUSH

Tom Walker

Sketches by Gretchen Walker

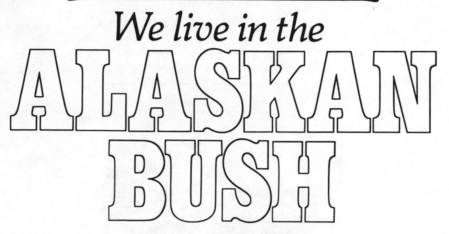

ALASKA NORTHWEST PUBLISHING COMPANY
ANCHORAGE, ALASKA

This book is dedicated to
Gretchen and Mary Anne
and to
the memory of Spencer A. Linderman,
who inspired me to write.

Library of Congress cataloging in publication data:
Walker, Tom, 1945-
    We live in the Alaskan bush.
    1. Walker, Tom, 1945-   2. McKinley, Mount, region, Alaska—Description and travel.   3. McKinley, Mount, region, Alaska—Biography.   I. Title.
F912.M2A35   979.8'3   77-17347
ISBN 0-88240-101-7

Design by Dianne Hofbeck
Diagrams by Jon.Hersh

Alaska Northwest Publishing Company
Box 4-EEE, Anchorage, Alaska 99509

Printed in U.S.A.

Contents

Preface

I first came to Loon Lake as an employee of the Alaska Department of Fish & Game. An Anchorage bush pilot, Jack Lee, flew me and my colleague Kirk McGee, along with a canoe and a variety of gear, in to the lake on a hot summer day. Loon Lake is located in the upper Susitna Valley at the foot of Mount McKinley, the mountain that the Indians call Denali—the high one. The views of McKinley, and of Mount Foraker and Mount Hunter, as we neared the lake were breath-taking. Moments before we touched down, a cow and calf moose splashed from the water and disappeared into the surrounding timber. Two trumpeter swans feeding at the far end of the lake, completely undisturbed by the approaching plane, flapped to an ungainly take-off only as we came to a gentle stop on the marshy shoreline.

Loon Lake was our destination because it is the headwaters of the Deshka River; we were to float the length of the river and count king salmon along the way.

The river winds for about 75 miles from the headwaters to the mouth, and at that time its upper reaches were undisturbed by man, so throughout our trip the wild creatures usually disregarded our canoe. That afternoon, just as we were ready to push off from shore, the cow and calf moose we had seen from the plane waded slowly back into the lake to feed. We watched as they bobbed their heads under the water to feed on succulent aquatic vegetation. While we observed the two moose, a strange call echoed across the forest as a loon gave voice to some wilderness emotion. I was suddenly aware of how good it felt to be in Alaska's back country again.

It took us six long days to float from Loon Lake to the mouth of the Deshka; the river was very low, and the journey arduous. We counted upward of 500 king salmon during the trip and encountered a variety of wildlife. River otters, black bears and bald eagles— those were only the beginning of the list of animals that we saw. The tracks and trails of beaver, muskrat and mink laced the muddy banks of the river. Occasionally a big moose would splash across the stream in front of us or crash off into the heavy underbrush that lined the bank.

As we traveled along I could not help feeling a sense of joy in the beauty and wildness of the country despite the long hours we put in each day. The idea of a home in the bush had always been of special interest to me, and during those six days land like that around Loon Lake made that idea seem more and more promising. By the end of our float a wilderness home in the Loon Lake region had become not an interest, but a goal. During the next few years my wife and I worked hard to reach that goal, and now we are able to call Loon Lake home. The road to our cabin in the woods has been a winding, difficult one—one rutted with moments of frustration and occasional hardship—but nonetheless it has been a very satisfying journey.

vii

1

Planning Ahead

I am a very fortunate man, because my wife, Gretchen, enjoys the outdoors and the wilderness as much as I do. In fact, I sometimes think she enjoys certain aspects of wilderness living more than I. She never complains about the inconveniences of living in the bush; whether it happens to be a log cabin we're living in, or a tent, she gets along just fine.

I had lived in Alaska three years before I met Gretchen. Like so many others before me, I was brought to Alaska by Uncle Sam's army. I had always planned on coming to Alaska anyway, so when the chance arose to fill my military obligation in Alaska, I took it.

I had lived in California before entering the service, working as a wrangler for a pack outfit in the Sierra Nevada Mountains, guiding dudes on hunting and fishing trips in the John Muir Wilderness Area. However, with its hundreds of people and their attendant piles of litter, the area hardly seemed to me to be wilderness and, as an incurable outdoorsman, I longed for the real thing: the Alaskan bush.

Gretchen was raised on a ranch in northern Nevada and the outdoors was very much a part of her family's life. Hiking, horseback riding, fishing and hunting were her family's shared activities, and when her father, an employee of the Federal Aviation Administration, was transferred to Alaska, she fitted right into the Alaskan scene. Clam digging, salmon fishing and berry picking came naturally as leisure-time activities.

We spent the first days of our marriage at Wolf Lake in the Nutzotin Mountains of eastern Alaska. I can remember hearing one night what sounded like a cattle stampede rushing by our tent and splashing off into the nearby lake. We both looked out just in time to see four moose go swimming rapidly across the lake, one a small bull. The next morning we found fresh grizzly tracks near the area where the moose had come from. It was a fine beginning for an Alaskan family.

A year after our marriage I found myself in Jack Lee's airplane headed for the Deshka River. When I returned home from that last salmon census of the season, I told Gretchen about the great area I had found along the river. After I concluded a lengthy but ungarnished description, she immediately launched into an equally long discussion of all the plans she had had for making a home in a wilderness cabin. She, too, had been longing for a life away from the conveniences of civilization. Now we are there. But as things worked out, it was to be a few years before we actually were able to make the move to the kind of life we really wanted.

"We're going to move to the bush," we would announce to our friends, and we were surprised to learn that many of them had the same ambition. As simple as it may seem at first, however, a family cannot just pull up roots and move to the woods. There is planning to be done, vital skills to be learned and money to be saved before anyone can acquire the independence necessary to get the feat accomplished. On top of it all, the determination must be total. We knew one couple that planned for six years to make such a move, and they seemed sincere in their goal, but in the end they went back to their home state of Colorado. They were rather typical of would-be bush dwellers.

Gretchen wanted to start building a cabin the next summer, but I convinced her that that was no way to start a new way of life. I knew of many cabins that had to be abandoned because the people who built them were unprepared for the rugged living involved. I also knew of some illegal cabins that had been burned by the U.S. Bureau of Land Management because they had been built in violation of the trespass law. That was because Alaska in the sixties had very little land available for purchase, and a person could not legally build a cabin just anywhere and move into it.

Our first step in the process of getting to the wilderness was to study maps of both federal and state lands that were available for homesteading or building.

*How to make a log house such as this one was among the things
I learned while preparing for our move from Fairbanks.*

At that time the area around Loon Lake was available for homesite development under the Alaska Open-to-Entry Program, which allowed a person to stake out and claim five acres of land for a home site or for a recreation area. (That program has been discontinued, however.)

By studying maps from the Division of Lands of the Alaskan Department of Natural Resources, I soon discovered that I would be a little late in staking property. A large amount of the best land available under the program, including several plots on Loon Lake, had already been claimed. I was disappointed by my discovery but nevertheless I snowshoed to the lake on the snowpack the following spring with my friend Jim Rothenbuhler to stake a claim. Even with the best spots already taken, I found, after some careful appraisal, a promising site. With Jim's help I measured off five acres and set the corner markers as required by law. When we returned to Fairbanks, where we were living at the time, I filed the necessary forms and paid the token fee. The land would be Gretchen's and mine on a five-year lease, which we could renew once. The law required that we have the land surveyed if we wished to buy it; once that was done, we could purchase the land at the price existing at the time of entry—that is, when Jim and I measured the five acres.

We had the survey made as soon as we could; then we purchased the land. That was exciting—owning those five acres meant that a dream was starting to come true.

Many writers of wilderness books give the impression that in order to live in the bush all one needs to do is merely move to a remote area, build a cabin, and live off the land. Simple. But, we asked ourselves, if living in the wilderness is that easy, why did we know so many people who had flunked out as far as this kind of life was concerned? For all of the years that I had lived in Alaska, I had spent as much time as possible in the woods, usually no less than three full months each year. One winter I trapped—with limited success—and almost every summer I worked the season for an outfitter. Yet, with as much outdoor living as I had done, I still had no real knowledge of what was necessary for the cabin we wanted to build. I could make a good hunting camp, yes, but there is a lot of difference between a real year-round home and a temporary place to hang your fishing or hunting equipment.

While living in Fairbanks, I worked as a commercial fisherman, newspaper writer, guide, carpenter and horse wrangler—to name a few of the many jobs I took to gain experience. I also worked for the Department of Fish & Game, and took courses at the University of Alaska in my spare time. All of these various projects were undertaken with an eye toward the life we would be living in the wilderness.

While gathering the necessary experience to enable us to move successfully to the bush, Gretchen and I tried to save money for the venture. Most people think that money is of little concern in the wilderness, but actually a person living in the woods becomes acutely aware of finances. There is little work available outside of the city and unless a person is a guide, a trapper or a commercial fisherman—all unstable seasonal occupations—or works for the government, there is little opportunity to earn an income. Items like air charter flights and the purchase and shipment of staples require a considerable cash outlay. Gretchen and I know several retired people who live successfully in the wilderness, but they have steady retirement incomes to keep them going. I have also known several trapper families who have lived in remote cabins for years, but in almost every case they have incomes from outside sources; some of them take weather observations for pay and others simply pack up and move to town for the summer months and go to work. We intended to make our wilderness home just that, a home, and that necessitated a stake. Like most people, however, we found saving money to be a difficult task.

If prior experience had taught us anything, it was that to be comfortable in the woods a family needs a good log cabin. I had some knowledge of building with logs but at best it was faulty. So, with a desire to gain valuable skills and experience working with logs, I went to work for Jim Smith, a Fairbanks log builder. Smith can be described as an artist with a chain saw and an ax. With those basic tools he creates beautiful log structures and homes. He has an eye for detail and each of his buildings is of high quality. I spent a fair portion of one summer working for Smith, and under his keen eye I quickly developed skills for practical log work, even though I had nowhere near his abilities.

Finally, after three years of planning, saving and picking up experience, we were ready to dive headfirst into the task of building our new home.

Meanwhile, life had taken on a new dimension in the form of a baby daughter, Mary Anne. We didn't let her arrival change our plans; she simply added one more element to the new kind of life we would soon be living.

2
The Beginning

Don Sheldon flew me in from Talkeetna to begin the arduous task of getting the cabin started. How many miles the flight covered I prefer not to say—Alaskan bush residents have developed a certain wariness about pinpointing the locations of their cabins. Too often, strangers have appeared at our doorsteps after reading about a life that seems to them to be exotic or romantic. Few of us are in the wild because we dislike people, certainly not me, but in the interests of privacy, I feel I cannot be specific about distances.

Don stayed only long enough to admire my 24-inch drawknife, inform me that he would be flying climbers back and forth to the mountains, and point out that I could lay a piece of bright material in a conspicuous spot if I needed any help. Then his floatplane roared overhead and I began moving my gear, tent and food to our home site. The distance to the site from the beaver house that served as a dock was not more than 300 yards, but after slogging along the shore with 12 loads of equipment, I felt the distance was a mile. I spent that entire first day carrying supplies and setting up camp.

The land had to be cleared, the site prepared and timber harvested and peeled. Originally, Gretchen had planned to accompany me on this first work trip, but her sister had arrived for a visit from the Lower 48, so I went to the lake alone.

The next morning I was up early and examining my proposed building site. I had chosen the spot carefully but there was a considerable amount of work to do before I could begin work on the cabin itself. I had selected a spot near the edge of our land on a slight rise that commanded a fine view of the mountains. It was solid, dry ground, and even a flood would not reach the site. I planned for the rear wall of the cabin to face south; with a window there, we could take advantage of what little sunlight there would be in winter. In addition, this would make the McKinley group clearly visible from our front porch.

The building site was overgrown with a heavy stand of alder and tenacious brush, but by noon I had the site cleared and ready for the piling holes. Many wilderness cabins are occasionally flooded by spring runoff or are dampened by overflow. Our site seemed reasonably secure from flooding, but I wasn't sure about the overflow problem; since a small spring bubbled nearby, we had decided to build the cabin on pilings. The finished product would then sit about 16 inches off the ground and be free of moisture problems. The use of pilings would also mean I could easily offset the slight slope at one corner of the site.

A gravel base lay only 18 to 20 inches below the surface and, since I wanted to set the pilings at least 6 feet deep, it took

Don Sheldon, who flew me in. He was famous for flying in Alaska's most rugged conditions.

me the rest of the day to dig the nine necessary holes. The next day I began the task of cutting timber and peeling logs. I figured that I would need about 45 trees; since the cabin would measure 16 by 18 feet on the inside, I could utilize some large spruce on the property and get two rounds, or rows, of logs from each tree, thereby reducing the number of trees that had to be cut.

The next five days were spent in hard labor. Each day I cut and peeled at least five house logs for the walls and roof and moved them to the site. Most of them were 10 to 12 inches across at the butt and, being green, they were exceedingly heavy and hard to move. Because the cabin style required an overhang on each end, and because saddle notching demands logs longer than the dimensions of the cabin, each log had to be 20 or 22 feet long. The ridgepole, cap logs and purlins, as well as the floor supports, were even longer, since the cabin was to have a roofed porch at the front end. (The ridgepole is the horizontal timber at the apex of the roof to which the upper ends of the roof rafters are attached; a cap log tops a wall, and a purlin is an intermediate roof support that runs from one gable to the other between, and parallel to, the cap log and the ridgepole.)

I used a come-along and a Handyman Jack to skid the logs the 50 or more yards to the site, and it took at least an hour to move each log. (A come-along is a hand-rachet winch; a Handyman Jack is a sturdy jack used for vehicles and heavy loads.) It would have been much less strenuous and time-consuming to use seasoned wood or standing dead timber, as I realized later.

After a long week of work, I had 15 peeled logs stacked on the site and another 15 logs cut, peeled and drying in the brush. It was a fairly good beginning, but to get such a start I had had to put in days of 14 and 16 hours. The weather was beautiful and sunny, but I had no time to enjoy the waterfowl that swam in the lake or the moose that often fed there at night.

With the preparatory work done, I was ready to sink the nine posts and proceed with the cabin construction. Working with logs 20 inches in diameter, I cut my posts 9 feet long, soaked them with creosote, and sank them into the holes I had dug. Next, using a chalk line and line level, I adjusted each post so that the top was level with the tops of all the others. For building supports I used three 30-foot logs that I had maneuvered to the site; each of these was cut and placed on three supporting posts. The three post-supported logs were parallel, 8 feet apart. The outer two logs, 16 feet apart, were the first layer of side logs, while the center log would function as a support for the floor and end walls. Using saddle notches (photo opposite and on page 29), I locked the entire project together by fitting two stout logs across and at right angles to the 30-footers. These two logs, spaced 18 feet apart, were the first rounds for the front and rear walls. The three 30-foot-long building-support logs were made to extend 10 feet in front of the front wall and 2 feet behind the rear wall. The extensions would help protect the foundation from the elements, and the front extension would eventually serve to support the front porch. When all were

On ground covered with sawdust, the cabin foundation takes shape.
This picture was taken from the front of the cabin.

pinned together, the two outside 30-foot logs and the two 16-foot end logs formed the 16- by 18-foot beginnings of the cabin.

It was almost midnight when I finished the preliminary log work, and after a late meal of canned chili and beans, I went to bed dog-tired. The night was overcast and still, giving me, and the mosquitoes, a respite from the 80-degree weather of the preceding days.

The next morning as I lay in my sleeping bag, I was sound asleep one moment and fully awake the next. I turned my head slowly and looked toward the tent entrance. There, not 30 inches away, a black bear stood peering in at me through the mosquito netting. I started to sit up but, with the quickness of a cat, the bear jumped away from the tent door and ran off into the surrounding brush. As I groped for my rifle, the sounds of the bear's retreat receded into the distance.

Waking up face to face with a black bear is an unnerving experience. I have

Side view of the cabin at the end of my first work trip. Log scraps to the right would come in handy later on for firewood.

never been able to figure out what caused me to awaken so abruptly; perhaps the bear had made some sound that I recognized unconsciously. I was awake enough to notice that the time was 4:20 a.m. and to be aware that the mosquitoes were keeping up their incessant droning outside the tent. Since the bear had departed, I looked around once and decided to go back to sleep. However, I took the precaution of loading my rifle and laying it close at hand.

One hour later I heard the sound of footfalls approaching my tent. I eased one arm out of my sleeping bag and grasped the rifle. The last thing I wanted to do was shoot the bear, but I knew that black bears could be dangerous and are not the clowns of the woods that some people think they are.

I sat up, rifle in hand, just in time to see the bear stretch up to look in the tent window. His ears were up at first, but when he saw me looking back at him, his ears laid back and a deep growl rumbled in his throat.

The roar of the rifle going off in the tent was deafening, but the shot in the neck from three feet away ended the bear's life without his knowing what had hit him. He fell against the tent.

With ringing ears I struggled to my feet. The echoes of the shot faded away and all was quiet except for the drone of the mosquitoes that quickly took advantage of the new hole in the bug netting and flew into the tent. Sleep had to be forgotten in the turmoil, and I quickly dressed and started making breakfast. I hadn't wanted to kill the inquisitive animal but felt I had had little choice.

The rest of the morning was spent skinning the bear and caring for the hide and meat. It was after lunch before I was able to get back to work on the cabin.

I had been seeing bear droppings and tracks around the lake since Don had dropped me off. After that first incident, my work area took on the air of a black-bear vacation spa. I saw bears almost every morning, but as soon as I began work they would move off. It is only the very rare bruin that causes trouble, but after being forced to shoot one of them, I took precautions to keep the camp as clean as possible and avoided anything that might offer temptations.

The cabin site is about 350 feet from the lake, and at that time the trail wound through heavy alder near the shoreline. One day I started down the trail to get a bucket of water and met yet another blackie. I entered the alder and crunched off noisily toward the lake. I had proceeded only a few yards when it dawned on me that I was making an unusually large amount of noise. I stopped abruptly in my tracks. Sure enough, something was following me and just after I stopped moving, whatever it was stopped moving, too. Again I took a few leaf-crunching steps forward, then halted. I repeated the process and the animal followed and stopped. I peered about trying to look at my companion but the heavy brush prevented me from seeing more than a few feet. Turning around, I faced the source of the noise and took several steps in place, crushing leaves underfoot. I stopped suddenly and watched as a much startled black bear hove into sight around a bend in the trail 40 feet away. The blackie came to a fast stop and stared at me in obvious surprise. The bear was a small one and had followed me out of youthful curiosity to see what manner of creature I was.

With outstretched arms I jumped a step at the little bear and yelled, "Gotcha!" Up went his long ears and with an expression that could only be described as shock the bear turned and fled up the trail.

After five more days of work, I had all my stacked logs adzed, notched and fitted into place. I knew the green logs would shrink and crack during the drying process; it certainly would have been better to have used seasoned logs.

When I quit work that first trip, the walls of the cabin were about 2½ feet high and ready for the floor to be put in. The two weeks of work had gone by smoothly and I had accomplished much;

15 logs lay in the woods drying and the cabin was rapidly taking shape. Except for the unexpected difficulty in moving the logs, I had proceeded about as well as planned. Don was due the next morning and so, on the 14th day, I packed and sorted equipment. The tent and some of the gear would be slung in a tree to await our return, while the rest of the gear and tools would go out on the flight with me. I had a cabin to work on for Jim Smith in Fairbanks before Gretchen and I would be free to resume construction on our own cabin. By afternoon I had finished moving to the beaver-house dock the gear I would take with me, and I sat down to enjoy the evening and the view of McKinley.

Suddenly I heard a loud splashing across the lake, and at the same time the grunting of large animals became audible. The sun was setting and the commotion was taking place directly in the brilliant glare that played on the water. The grunting sounds grew louder as a cow and calf moose swam out from the glare and headed straight across the lake toward me. The calf was reddish brown and very small, but it kept up easily with the rapidly moving cow. I soon realized that another animal was making huffing sounds, and a loud splash announced the arrival of a third swimmer. I could not at first see the newcomer because of the glare, but soon a grizzly came into sight, paddling furiously after the two fleeing moose.

The cow and calf had passed the midway point in the lake when the bear began to slow down. The grizzly was visibly tiring and the two moose were widening their lead. They soon reached shore and steamed off into the trees not 50 yards away from me. The grizzly had not yet arrived at the halfway point when it turned in a wide arc and started back.

The bear swam with effort toward the far bank and before he reached dry ground his dog paddle was decidedly labored. He climbed out of the water and shook himself like a dog, took a long look around, sniffed at the ground, and walked slowly into the forest.

The sun sank below the forested horizon and the amber glow faded to twilight. The night was perfectly still and, except for the occasional riffles where a rainbow trout broke the surface to snatch an insect, the lake was mirrorlike. An occasional muskrat or beaver swam by on a night prowl for food, its wake trailing behind. The mountain range faded, a great horned owl hooted, and feeding waterfowl quieted as the seminight of summer came on.

The next morning Don arrived on time and we were soon airborne, but I'll long remember sitting there, absorbing the sights and sounds of the forest at the place where our new home would be.

13

3
Sights and Sounds of Fall

The rest of the summer raced by, and soon I was back at Loon Lake. The waning days of September ushered in a beautiful Indian summer of cloudless days and crisp nights. The gold, yellow and red of autumn covered the paper-birch forest that surrounded our cabin site. Gretchen and I, along with one-year-old Mary Anne, camped on the site as the tedious work of notching and fitting logs progressed.

A friend came out to spend a weekend with us and to look for a moose to line his freezer. The good-natured friend never even saw a moose, but he volunteered for some back-breaking labor and helped me carry in the logs that had been drying all summer. The going was very difficult, but once we got a log up on our shoulders we managed to stumble the 50 or 60 yards to the cabin site before putting it down. We had no way of estimating the weight of each log, but we found that carrying one proved to be a lot faster than moving it with a come-along. Our friend's brief stay ended with a memorable afternoon of photographing waterfowl; then Don Sheldon whisked our helper back to civilization.

Our small family was finally alone in the bush and doing what we had long planned for. Each day Gretchen and the baby would wander about the forest, Gretchen enjoying the fall colors and sketching, while I worked on the cabin.

In three days I had all the logs up that had been carried in, and the cabin walls stood 4½ feet high. The days were still warm, but the nights were growing colder—a reminder that winter would be soon at hand.

On one of those chilly late-fall mornings I woke up early. Through the open tent flap I could see that the sky, which had been a clear blue the previous evening, had turned a sullen gray. As I got up I could hear the splashing sounds of ducks and the louder, raucous calls of the lesser Canada geese. Occasionally I would hear the eerie cry of a loon.

Above all others came the calls of the trumpeter swans. The trumpeters had been gathering for several days, and their splashing games and off-key trumpeting were fascinating accompaniments to our daily activities. A week earlier only two swans had been in the lake, but as I

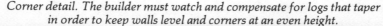

Corner detail. The builder must watch and compensate for logs that taper in order to keep walls level and corners at an even height.

15

approached the lakeshore that morning I counted a flock of 22 birds, only one of them wearing the somber gray plumage of immaturity.

A light mist rose above the lake. Long fingers of ice reached out from shore, and soon the harsh winter would come and the lake would freeze over. Beyond the thin ice, muskrats swam back and forth with grass clamped in their mouths. When winter came, the industrious rodents would have to build their push-ups through the ice. Unlike their cousins, the beavers, who cache their food under the ice, the muskrats must forage for food daily, and the push-ups are their doors to the world from their icebound lodges.

The morning mist was fanned away by a freshening breeze. Overhead a golden eagle circled, then folded its wings and dived toward a group of feeding golden-eyes. The alarmed ducks splashed off and landed beside some feeding swans, seeming to seek protection. The eagle altered its direction and continued toward the ducks, but as the ducks approached the swans, the golden spread its wings, pulled out of its dive, and disappeared over the trees.

From a grass-covered blind I had built on the lakeshore, I watched the feeding trumpeter swans. The swans feed much as

Morning freezeup whitens Loon Lake. Mount Hunter and Mount McKinley are in background.

puddle ducks do, tipping up to feed on submerged vegetation. Occasionally, as one swan would tip up, another would suddenly reach out and nip the upthrust tail. Surfacing with a great splash and gurgling trumpet, the offended bird, outraged at the indignity, would chase the joker away. While most of the flock fed quietly, others floated along in pairs, facing each other now and again and bobbing their heads up and down, alternately emitting loud calls.

Slowly the early morning bustle stilled and I returned to work on the cabin. Walking up the trail to camp, I saw a pine grosbeak flit through the woods, lighting long enough to sample a highbush cranberry. None of these brilliant red, robin-size finches had been near camp for some time. This one obviously was passing through on its migration south.

About noon the skies darkened, and to the north the lower flanks of Mount McKinley, which had been visible under the overcast, faded from sight. Overhead, in seemingly endless streams, great wedges of geese flew by, their calls ringing across the spruce-birch forest. Blending with the answering trumpets of the swans, the cries of the wild geese made a concerto of the wild.

Early in the afternoon, more swans arrived in groups of two and three. Their distant trumpeting announced their approach, and long before they landed,

*A rare visitor, a big Canada goose, looks lost on
the ice of the early-frozen lake.*

the birds on the water greeted them with welcoming calls.

My work, interrupted several times as I gazed at the panorama in the sky, stopped completely with the arrival of a long-tailed weasel. The sinewy brown-and-yellow animal had been living near our building site for some time, and he darted quickly through the grass and showed no fear as he searched for crumbs in and around the tent. Leaving him to his hunt, I laid down my tools and headed for the lake.

As the clouds lowered even more, the north wind increased. Ancient 60-foot birches along the lakeshore groaned and shrieked from the force of the wind. Looking out over the lake, I saw a few stray swans still feeding, but most of the great flock had gathered at the north end, calling in a new, more strident trumpet. I shivered in my down jacket as the wind howled with growing force. Suddenly the flock formed and, with a great splashing, the white swans rose as a group, banked away from the north wind and were gone. Their calls were lost in the distance, and stillness settled on the lake.

With a sense of loss, I turned away from the water. As I moved toward camp, the first big flakes of wind-driven snow began to pelt the lake. Winter had come.

Soon we ourselves would have to leave; we were not yet ready to spend our first winter in the bush.

4

Meeting Our Neighbors

The cabin we had had in mind (no blueprint existed) was the traditional Alaskan trapper-style design. Common throughout Alaska, the trapper's cabin features a low-pitched roof, low walls and a front overhang that shelters a porch. The roof is usually supported by five logs: the ridgepole, two cap logs and two purlins. Some variations of the design end up with double ridgepoles or with four purlins, two on each side of the ridgepole. The double-ridgepole design is used in areas with small-diameter logs that aren't sturdy enough to serve as single ridgepoles. Our roof features the standard five-log support system, all of the poles extending far enough in front of the cabin to shelter the porch. This traditional design evolved because such a cabin could easily support a heavy ridgepole, a sod roof and a hefty load of snow, even though the roof was not steeply pitched.

The basic design was born of practicality. The original pioneers in Alaska heated and cooked almost exclusively with wood; in a climate distinguished by long winters and temperatures that drop regularly to 40 degrees below zero and more, a cabin had to be snug and require a minimum amount of firewood. The only major alteration that we made in the proved design was to replace the pole-and-sod roof with one of plywood and tar paper. The old-timers built roofs of small-diameter spruce poles that were laid next to each other and ran from a ridgepole to the cap logs. Such a roof was covered with sod. On a cabin the size of the one we were building, I estimated that it would take almost 150 saplings to make the poles for the roof. For that reason we abandoned the idea of a pole roof; we did not want to denude our land. As it turned out, the roof style we chose proved to be ideal; in fact, when the outside temperature is 10 degrees or warmer, a small fire in the stove easily heats the entire cabin, and at times the door has to be opened a crack to allow cool air to circulate.

On my travels around Alaska, I have seen the trapper-style cabin in many different locations and in use by many different kinds of people. Modern outdoorsmen find the design as practical as the old-timers did. Hunters of the early mining days, as well as the miners they served, used it. Trappers and prospectors in the remote Brooks Range built small cabins on the basic design, and so did commercial fishermen in Southeastern Alaska, at the opposite end of the state. Some of these old cabins are still in use today, testifying to their strength.

It was the early fur trappers, however, who originated the style of cabin that carries their name. Old cabins found in prime fur country in widely scattered parts of Alaska look almost as though they were all built by the same person. The lonely trappers led difficult lives and their rugged handiwork shows it. The cabins were always built for warmth and protection from the elements; most were located in stands of heavy timber to be protected from the wind and also to be near building materials and firewood. Small windows and, sometimes, roofs with two layers of poles aided in heat retention. More recent bush cabins feature high steeply peaked roofs, often with lofts. Heating these cabins is sometimes a problem, although the lofts are a good idea. In any case, the trapper-style cabin has been time-tested and has proved to be a quality product, and that is why we adopted the design.

After I started work on the cabin we stayed one more winter in town. If I had been able to work straight through that first summer on the construction, we would easily have been able to finish the cabin. However, prior commitments, not to mention a one-year-old daughter and all that she involved, prohibited a move just then. That first summer I spent a few days less than a full month—two two-week trips—working on the cabin.

Prepipeline Fairbanks, where we were living, was a nice place to be if we couldn't live in the bush, weather notwithstanding. We had a small cabin some miles from the main part of town and escaped much of the ice fog and the problems of the city. What made Fair-banks a pleasant place to live in at that time was the unique collection of people who called the town home: trappers, miners, hunters, wildlife photographers, loggers and dog mushers. Fairbanks still retained the feel of a small town on the edge of a great frontier.

A mystifying situation occurred that winter in Fairbanks that favorably affected our purchases for the bush cabin. Consumer goods and services have always been more expensive in that interior city than elsewhere because of the high cost of shipping. A bargain hunter who was really intent on saving money could drive 358 miles to Anchorage and make a major purchase at substantial savings despite the cost of the trip. When it came time for us to buy the building materials for the cabin—plywood, tar paper and insulation—we compared Anchorage and Fairbanks prices, naturally expecting those in Anchorage to be cheaper, and were surprised to find that the things we needed cost less in Fairbanks. We have been unable to figure out why unless costs were low due to the depressed economy in Fairbanks prior to the pipeline boom.

To avoid the high cost of air trans-portation, I had planned to haul building materials to Loon Lake by snow machine and sled, a project that would involve several round trips. A friend volunteered the use of his two snow machines, as well as the sleds to attach behind them, and he and I began the job of hauling materials from the newly completed Anchorage-Fairbanks Highway (now the George Parks Highway).

The going was difficult at first, and we wasted one entire day without ever reaching the cabin site. The machines constantly broke through the crust and bogged down. Once we got a trail packed, however, the sledding proved easier. Still, on slight hills and rises we had to stop and unpack the sleds and carry the lumber and materials uphill, one piece at a time. Then we had to repack the sleds and start again. After five tough days of sledding, I had three-quarters of the building materials at the cabin site. We should have been able to get all of the materials in with the two snow machines, but one of them blew a head gasket and our sledding came to an abrupt halt.

After the friend returned to town with the sleds and a repaired machine, I remained at the cabin and cut the rest of the trees necessary for the cabin and moved them to the site. Skidding logs over the snow proved to be a lot easier than moving them in summer, but still the process was a slow show for one man. However, in three days I had all the logs I needed for the cabin cut and hauled.

As I machined out from the lake, the trail showed signs of melting under the

Trumpeter swans, surely some of our most elegant neighbors, are also among the friendliest and most inquisitive.

warm sun, and I knew that spring was getting close.

Spring comes to the north in a frenzy of rebirth. Suddenly the land seems tired of the monotony of white, and the northern forests shed their winter shroud in a blaze of brilliant warm days. Signaling the return of summer are the cries of wild birds and—protected from human eyes and ears—the wobbling steps of moose calves and the squalls of bear cubs. The transition from winter to spring is a short one, or seems to be, when compared to the drab days that herald the approach of winter. It is a thankful land and people that welcome the sun on its northward journey.

After a long winter the spring found us back at the lake and hard at work. The walls of the cabin went up fast and our new home rapidly took shape, thanks in part to spectacular weather. The spring was a glorious one, with little rain. Because of the prolonged dryness, biting insects were minimal and we were grateful for the absence of mosquitoes.

We probably could have finished the cabin more quickly than we did, but our animal neighbors proved too interesting to ignore. Trumpeter swans, otters, black bears and moose are the most visible wild inhabitants of the environs of the lake. During the cabin construction, hardly a day went by without an encounter with wild visitors. We took time out from work to watch and enjoy our neighbors.

The swans are the most obvious inhabitants of the area. Because of their trumpeting and their habitat on the open lake, we are more aware of them than the creatures of the forest. At times the swans exhibit considerable curiosity, either being very friendly or just plain inquisitive. When one of us ventures near the lake, the swans, usually a pair but sometimes more, spot the movement and swim toward it. Occasionally when spying one of us, a swan will let out a loud trumpet. If someone sends back an imitation of the call, the birds will really get into gear and steam over to investigate.

Whenever Gretchen goes to the lake to get water or to sit and watch the wildlife, the swans swim over, usually no closer than 10 yards, and sit in the water craning their long necks to watch her and our daughter. Mary Anne has learned to call the swans and her squeaky voice imitating them almost always gets an instant response from the big birds. They often answer with a cacophony of calls among themselves and can be kept going by an occasional imitation. The visit rarely ends with the swans swimming away, but rather with the departure of the human visitor. For some time after one of these encounters we can hear the swans calling and see them floating in the same area as if waiting for a friend's return.

The white birds' behavior is in marked contrast to that of other waterfowl. To get close to ducks or geese for photos, an elaborate blind is needed and a photographer must use caution. With swans, however, the quicker the movements of the person on the shore, the more interested they seem to be. It has occurred to us that the birds have become accustomed to people feeding them at refuges in the south. In any case, most of the swans at Loon Lake have no fear of us at all.

Swans nest in our lake and in adjacent lakes but they don't seem to be successful at rearing their young. The first fall we worked on the cabin, we had about 30 swans on the lake—the largest number that we have ever seen—yet only one was a cygnet. I found a trumpeter's nest one summer and broken eggs were mute evidence of what had happened: a mink or other predator had gotten the eggs before they could hatch. For a rare bird like the trumpeter swan, whose habitat is steadily shrinking, this is one of nature's tragedies.

Otters, which belong to the weasel family, are abundant along the upper Deshka and its headwaters, and we see them often. One day Gretchen, after getting a pail of water, was sitting on the dock when she noticed an otter swimming uncertainly toward her. The otter swam to within 35 feet. Then, with a peculiar coughing bark, it submerged, resurfaced a few feet away, and coughed

An appealing pair—but a photographer who gets too close probably will encounter their mother.

again. The graceful animal peered at her for several minutes, trying to figure out what manner of creature sat on the bank. After several more barks, it was satisfied and swam away.

In the cool evenings of summer when the sun sets late and the sky is still bright, otters can be seen swimming through the lily pads in their search for food. Fresh-water mussels abound in the muddy depths of Loon Lake and broken shells along the bank testify to the otters' ability to harvest mollusks. Otters also eat fish. They probably catch rainbow trout, and in late summer go downstream to feed on spawned-out or dead salmon.

Black bears come into our area regularly in their search for anything edible, usually causing no trouble and providing an interesting break from the daily schedule. However, bears routinely tear up the garbage dump in their quest for food, so, to keep them from becoming dependent on garbage, we make it a point to burn the contents of the garbage pit every time it is used. The burning keeps the problem to a minimum, but the bears still scavenge for scraps. One morning just after I had cut the door and windows into the cabin, we were awakened by a loud thump on the cabin wall. From inside the cabin we looked up to see an enormous black bear—one of the biggest I've ever seen—peering in the window above our heads. He had both paws on the sides of the window and his huge nose quivered as he sorted out the various smells issuing from inside. I sat up just as the bear dropped to the ground and lumbered away. Although he stayed around for three days, he never caused us any trouble.

Moose feed in the lake at night. On evenings after I have been using the chain saw, however, the moose will not come, but if we are relatively quiet at our daytime tasks, moose emerge with the twilight and feed on aquatic plants.

The area around us is not prime moose country because it lacks good winter browse. Heavy forests of spruce-birch predominate, with very little of the willow that is a mainstay of a moose's diet; in winter, when the snow is four feet deep or more, there is little for the moose to eat and wintering becomes difficult. As with many types of wildlife, the winter range for moose is an important factor in limiting their numbers. We have found that in winter the moose travel from big tree to big tree and feed on the exposed brush and grass that is sheltered by overhanging limbs. The summer browse, however, is almost unlimited for the number of moose in the area, and, except for the mosquitoes that bother them, the big deer, having struggled through the difficult winter, have an easy time in summer.

5

Building the Cabin

Building with logs qualifies as manual labor of the most strenuous variety. With only one person working, it is doubly hard, especially handling and moving the logs. Maneuvering the house logs proved to be the most difficult part of the construction of the cabin. A 22-foot-long green or partly dried log is by no means light, and Gretchen just wasn't strong enough to help lift the logs into place. Once the cabin walls were 4 feet high, it was difficult to lift the remaining logs off the ground and onto a wall. Our come-along proved to be of immense value in getting the last few logs up and into place on the wall (diagram 1).

The bottom round of logs on two sides of the cabin has floor joists on it, leaving a space between the bottom log and the rest of the wall logs. To raise a log on a wall opposite that space, I passed the come-along anchor rope through the space and tied the rope around the base log. (For the other two walls the anchor rope was simply fastened to a joist.) I lifted one end of a log as high as I could up to the wall where it was to go, bracing it at the top with wedges. Then I would pull out the winch cable from the come-along and attach the hook at the end of the cable to the low end of the log. This way I could easily crank the log off the ground and up onto the wall. Using the

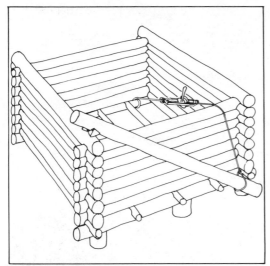

Diagram 1: *Using the Come-along to Lift Logs —
The rope from the come-along was anchored to
the bottom log of the opposite wall or to a floor
joist. The log to be raised was lifted as high as
possible, then braced with wedges. The hook
from the come-along cable was attached to the
low end of the log, which could now be cranked
up into place.*

hand winch enabled me to avoid the
time-consuming process of building and
arranging a set of skid ramps each time a
new log went up. The finished wall was a
little over 5½ feet high.

I used saddle notches to fit the logs
together. Saddle notching is a fast way to
fit logs, and the finished product provides
a watertight joint. My method of laying a
round was the simple and efficient one
that I had learned from Jim Smith in
Fairbanks. First, with the log on the wall, I

rolled it until I had the flattest and
smoothest side face down, then I lightly
marked that side with chalk for identi-
fication and rolled the log over until the
marked side was up. I made a chalk line
the length of the log and, using that
straight line as a guide, ran the chain saw
along it, adzing flat a bearing surface 2 to
3 inches wide. The log then could be
turned flat side down and moved into the
approximate place it would fit after
notching.

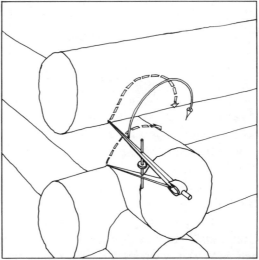

Diagram 2: *Marking a Log for a Saddle Notch —
A divider is used for a scribe. When a curve is
drawn on a log to be notched, the scribe must be
held firmly so the legs remain in place. Starting at
one side of the bottom log, the scribe is moved up
and over to the other side. The sharp point of the
top leg of the scribe will mark the top log,
showing where the notch is to be cut.*

A finished saddle notch. This log is now ready to be rolled over and fitted onto the log underneath it.

Using a pair of dividers as a scribe, I marked the notches to be cut out (diagram 2). The distance between the two points of the scribe—usually the radius of the lower log—determines the height of the notch. Having set the scribe, and always keeping the legs of the scribe the same distance apart, I followed the curve of the lower log with the low point of the scribe while keeping the upper point pressed tightly to the upper log. The resulting mark on the top log corresponded perfectly with the shape of the lower log. Once a notch was marked at each end, the log was turned over and the notches cut out with the tip of the chain saw.

After the notches were cut, each log was carefully turned over and fitted into place. Usually the notches fitted correctly and the adzed areas were tight. Sometimes, however, high spots kept the logs apart and the notches from fitting together properly. Then I had to mark the high spots and adz them down. The logs usually fitted fine after remedial

*With her rag doll for company, Mary Anne takes a nap
in a nest of shavings in spite of the building activity nearby.*

treatment but on occasion a log had to be reworked twice.

After setting it into proper position, I finished the round by repeating the adzing procedure on the top side of the log. Before the logs were pinned together a strip of fiberglass insulation was laid between the adzed areas, providing the only insulation used between the logs.

Many log structures are built with the logs spiked together. From examining such cabins I have learned that logs do need some inner bracing, but to merely drive in a spike without first drilling a hole for it should be avoided because the logs shrink as they dry. The spikes then hold the logs apart and keep them from settling properly. The result is that the notches don't fit as tightly as possible and, of course, the logs need to be rechinked.

The alternative to spiking is drilling and pegging. In the bush, without electricity, that involves a great deal of hand labor. Pegging, or pinning, the logs together is a simple task with an electric auger, but when the holes have to be tapped by hand the work is monumental. The extra effort is worth it, however, for a properly pinned cabin settles tightly and is much warmer than a spiked cabin. Rebars (steel reinforcing rods) are the most commonly used wall pins in some areas, but I have found that wooden pegs are best. When it comes time to cut out a

door or window, the builder who has used wooden pins instead of steel ones does not have to worry about hitting metal with his saw. We hand-drilled the holes in our logs and set the pegs in with a sledge. If we had had a portable generator and electric drill we could have saved ourselves a lot of work and time.

Most old bush cabins that I have seen, and some town cabins too, bulge conspicuously at the walls near windows and doors. That usually means that the windows and doors were cut out of the walls and then framed in without any additional inner bracing. The bowing comes with time as the logs settle and exert pressure on the openings. To avoid this problem, a spline, usually cut from a two-by-two or a two-by-four, can be fitted into a slot cut vertically into the log ends on each side of window and door openings. This added strength ties the logs together on each side of the opening and prevents bowing (diagram 3; photo, page 32). I used the tip of the chain saw blade to cut out the slots for the splines in our cabin and found this to be an excellent method for making slots.

From the day the first tree was cut, 5½ weeks' total building time had gone into construction; now we were ready to put up the ridgepole. Gretchen and I knew it would be impossible to put up the ridgepole by ourselves so a young friend, Bill Basinski, came out to help us set the

31

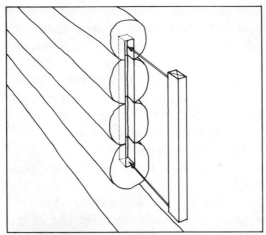

Diagram 3: *A Window Spline — A two-by-two or a two-by-four is fitted into each side of a window opening to provide strength and prevent bulging as settling occurs. Now that this window opening has been neatly splined, it's ready for the frame to be put in place.*

ridgepole and put the roof on. The 28-foot-long ridgepole had been drying for over a year and we had little trouble setting the log in place. We made use of the come-along and got the ridgepole up onto the building in much the same manner as the wall logs went up. Bill and I spent the next two days cutting the gables and putting the roof on. With that, the majority of the heavy work was finished, and what was left was easy. An entry in my diary detailed that day.

> Up at 5:30. No bear this morning. Bill and I start laying plywood and by noon the roof is on. Hot and sunny today. Few mosquitoes. Bill good worker and cheerful. Roof is on and looks good—nice green color. Finish door in late afternoon. Only two mistakes on roof, one high spot, one low spot. Not bad, though. Quit early at 6:30.

We had a cabin! It lacked some finishing touches, but it was a house, and it was ours, and it meant the beginning of a new kind of life.

Another project accomplished during Bill's stay was the final work on the cabin door, which was built for strength first, with decorative value a secondary consideration. A cabin door needs to fit tightly to guard against heat loss in winter and to prevent the entry of biting insects in summer. With an eye to strength, I built the cabin door out of sections of two-by-six tongue-and-groove decking that I had glued and clamped together. For decorative exterior support I used some hand-trimmed two-by-fours in a Z design; the two-by-four crosspieces were bolted to the decking and added considerable strength. Big sturdy strap hinges were used to hang the heavy door, and a simple metal thumb latch was fitted as a handle and lock. Finally, for practical as well as ornamental value, I bolted a big caribou shovel to the door to serve as a handle. The finished product

Ridgepole, purlin and cap log in place.

turned out to be sturdy and attractive (photo, page 65).

If a small bush cabin is to be practical, furnishings must be carefully thought out in advance. There is only so much living area, and space-saving designs and dual-purpose construction are important. Storage and shelving space are at a premium, so to get the most out of the available space I made both Mary Anne's bed and ours high enough off the floor to allow utilization of the space underneath. Built into the space under Mary Anne's bed is a large crawl-in toy box. Not only does it serve her for storage, it also serves as a play area. Under our bed is a 32-inch-high storage area with a box for fresh produce and with shelves for our clothes and miscellany. The storage area

Mary Anne sits on our bed, which is also the top of the clothes box. Wall space is used for shelves, and the end of the bed is a bookcase.

is high enough so that we can also hang clothes on a built-in rack.

Gretchen's and my combination bed-storage area was built in the left-hand back corner of the cabin. Above the bed I augered four holes and drove in hand-hewn pegs on which I placed two shelves for bric-a-brac. Mary Anne's bed-toy box went in the back right-hand corner, where a peg-supported shelf holds her book collection. Above and around her bed, I fashioned a wire slide on which Gretchen hung curtains that can be drawn when Mary Anne's bedtime rolls around.

In the front right-hand corner of the cabin went a big airtight wood stove with two drying shelves on each side. Because cabin fires are all too common in Alaska, and because most of these fires are caused by overheated wood stoves, I built a fire-prevention device for the stove out of some scrap plywood and logs. By fitting small log ends onto a rectangular piece of plywood, I built a box that we filled with five inches of dirt. The stove legs rest on the dirt, and any sparks or hot ashes that fall from the stove land on the soil and die out.

I spent two days building a counter with a cupboard underneath it in the left-hand corner of the cabin by the front window. The cupboard has large doors to give easy access to the spacious shelving. After staining the cupboard, I covered the top with a heat-resistant material.

Just inside the door on the left went a washstand with shelves underneath. An old-fashioned pitcher and basin serve for washing, and a round tub that can be placed beside the wood stove is our bathtub.

Next to the cupboard I installed an old wood-burning cookstove that I had hauled in by snow machine the preceding winter. The old Harmony had been salvaged from some neighbors when we lived in Fairbanks. The unit had been badly rusted in places, so for $22 we had had a sheet-metal shop replace the legs, build a new ash box and weld the top plates. The old stove has proved to be of immense value and the little oven has turned out fresh breads, cookies and other delectable baked goods.

I made a medicine chest out of a crate that once held containers of white gas and hung it on the wall. To complete our furnishings I built a table from dried spruce boards and poles. The finished table went in the middle of the cabin (diagram 4).

Gretchen made some attractive red hand-stitched curtains for the windows. As a last touch we covered two-thirds of the floor with a rust-colored rug—a valuable addition because it covers the cold boards and helps retain warmth.

Since we planned to use wood both to heat the cabin and to cook, we needed a good supply of firewood. Getting firewood

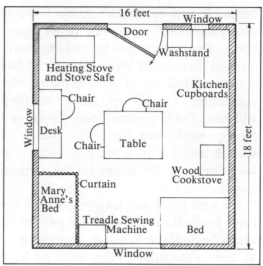

Diagram 4: *Floor Plan of the Cabin.*

has been no problem at all. A cabin-building project soon accumulates a stack of ends, butts and waste that makes great firewood. When we first began work on the cabin, two dead spruce and a large dead birch were removed from the building site and cut up into firewood lengths. While Bill Basinski was with us, he and I cut and stacked firewood and ended up with an enormous pile, some of which we used immediately, the rest being left to dry further.

For us, spruce makes the ideal firewood; it is excellent for starting fires and burns and ignites faster than birch. Birch seems to have a high degree of moisture retention and needs a long drying period before it can be used. But birch burns slowly and evenly, and once we get a good spruce fire crackling in the heating stove, we add sections of birch. We try to use spruce exclusively in the Harmony—the cookstove. A good armload of kindling will keep the cookstove going for several hours, while two good-size pieces of spruce, along with a piece of birch, will burn brightly for hours in the airtight heating stove.

As with most building projects of the do-it-yourself variety, our cabin will never really be finished. We keep improving, or at least changing, things until we have remedied a discomfort or problem. I even rebuilt our bed in an effort to use the space better. However, even though the construction and furnishings may be rough in places, our cabin is warm and comfortable.

Looking back on it all, we can, inevitably, see mistakes we made in building the cabin, and things we would have done differently. Specifically, I would have waited until winter to haul my logs, because then I could have used the snow machine. Instead of using green logs I would have used dead standing timber, which is dry, light, and easier to handle. I would have built the roof steeper to shed water and snow more efficiently and I would have made the cabin walls a bit higher. So much for hindsight. In spite of mistakes, it was all well worth the sweat and effort.

6
A Wilderness Childhood

Mary Anne has been a child of the wilderness almost since the day she was born—in fact, since before she was born, for I have a picture of Gretchen, seven months pregnant, hiking in the high sheep country of the Alaska Range. When Mary Anne was less than two weeks old, she and Gretchen flew to a wilderness camp where I was working 60 air miles from Fairbanks and 40 miles from any road. That early bush flight may very well have given her an incurable love of flying. She still "helps" fly airplanes whenever she gets the chance and wishes she were in the air any time a plane flies over us.

Mary Anne was a cradle-board baby; from the time she was a few days old until she was nearly four months old, she rode on her mother's back strapped in her moosehide papoose board. The Indian-style cradle board, with attached shoulder straps, proved to be a good way to carry her and also served as a great portable crib. Punkin, as we sometimes call Mary Anne, has also been a camper for all her short life. When we were building the cabin she slept in the tent with us, snuggling into her own miniature sleeping bag that Gretchen had made by hand. Early one fall morning a black bear approached the tent, attracted by camp odors and looking for scraps. Mary Anne chose that particular moment to wake up and, as usual, she awoke noisily. The bear disappeared with amazing speed. In that

Mary Anne at two weeks, in her cradle board.

Fairbanks, where we lived when Mary Anne was still tiny, there was a formidable array of photos, paintings and books of wild sheep as well as one mounted Dall ram head. Little wonder that *sheep* replaced *Daddy* as the second word of Mary Anne's vocabulary. Almost all her favorite picture books are collections of wildlife photos. She was quite young when she first learned to recognize pictures of animals and point out the moose, caribou and bears. Mary Anne can sit for long periods in her mother's lap with books, pointing out different animals, but the wild mountain sheep is still her favorite. Many times a day she gets her picture books out, or a *National Geographic,* and sits looking at the pictures. On walks about the lake, we have been amazed that she so readily recognizes some of our wild neighbors.

Above all else, we hope to teach our daughter a love for the wilderness and the wild creatures that inhabit it. We don't want her to learn Hollywood-style concepts about wildlife but prefer, rather, to let her see and learn the ways of animals firsthand. Anthropomorphic, humanized animals, as portrayed by Walt Disney and other contemporary storytellers, bear little resemblance to real animals. We hope that Mary Anne will learn to respect and love wildlife but at the same time will realize that hunting wildlife for food is one aspect of sound conservation.

old bruin's life, he had probably been chased by grizzlies, annoyed by rut-crazed moose and harrassed by hunters, but a squalling one-year-old baby girl was just too much for him.

The second word our daughter uttered—of course *Mama* was the first—was *sheep.* I have long had an interest in mountain sheep and have studied them and their habits for years. In our house in

Many people have asked us what we intend to do when Mary Anne reaches school age. That is a difficult question to answer, but if our life style remains much as it is now, we intend to teach her ourselves with the aid of a home-study correspondence plan. We have known many bush parents who have been quite successful in educating their own children. We do realize, however, that home study is not simple. A home-study program could be easily put aside or deviated from, and a strict schedule and plans have to be established and followed. Teaching at home does offer the advantages of a one-to-one relationship and a curriculum designed to fit individual aptitudes. A tight family bond can develop as well as close supervision over the child.

We also realize that children require the company of other children so that they can learn to function socially. This appears to be the major disadvantage of having a lone child in the bush. We have always made it a point when in town to visit Mary Anne's friends, as well as our own. In the cabin she seems to be able to last about one month, sometimes less, before she needs the company of other people. Whenever friends come to see us, Mary Anne is delighted.

One difficulty we have encountered in living in the bush is that of finding enough to keep a child occupied. Many times we find our daughter needing something to do besides getting into everything she shouldn't. Axes and saws are not toys, but it takes a while for her to get the message that there are some things she has to stay away from. Each day we try to devote at least two hours exclusively to her. Sometimes Gretchen takes her for long walks or pulls her in the sled; we've found that every outing proves to be a lesson. Mary Anne could identify the peculiar sliding trail of an otter and the hopping tracks of a marten when she was only 2½. Occasionally I take her for hikes to show her the moose that feed not far from the cabin or, in summer, swans that feed in the lake. One of the most enjoyable experiences Gretchen and I ever had was seeing the look of wonder on Mary Anne's face the night the sky was illuminated by an intense display of northern lights and she saw the aurora for the first time. Our daughter's life may be marked by the absence of companionship with youngsters her own age, but on the other hand she certainly has no lack of stimulating and interesting experiences in what to us is the real world.

The wilderness is a wonderful school not only for our child but for Gretchen and me as well. There are many lessons to learn and fascinating wildlife activities to observe. Each fall migrating waterfowl bring their vitality to our lake. One late

Bath time in the wilderness: a portable tub works fine.

September day a cold wind laced across the water and, although the sky was clear, the noon temperature stood unyieldingly at 25 degrees. A thin crust of ice crept out from shore and gripped most of the lake surface in a chilly embrace. Rafted together in the center of the lake, groups of lesser Canada geese, mallards and widgeons floated and milled about. Earlier in the day the last flights of green-winged teal had left on their journey south. Alaskan waterfowl leave the state in muted, mottled colors with merely a hint of the real beauty of their mature plumage. Only as the autumn wears on and the birds move southward does their plumage fully mature; then the last vestige of the eclipse plumage gives way to the brilliant hues familiar to people who see waterfowl farther south.

The ducks that rafted together in the icy waters that day were of many different species, yet I had difficulty identifying individual birds because of their dreary plumage. Even males and females were almost identical and we found that we had to look for subtle color differences in order to tell them apart. Earlier in the summer, before the molt, we had had little difficulty in distinguishing the different breeds and sexes.

Several types of waterfowl summer at our lake, swans, of course, being the most conspicuous. Other resident species include buffleheads, scaups, mallards and pintails. The latter two are dabbling ducks—those that tip up to feed—while the others are bottom-feeding divers. A few of the smallest of all dabblers, the green-winged teal, are also summer residents.

In early summer the lake is home to the courting waterfowl that nest along the shore. Near the high grass and brush that line the lake and feeder streams, drakes cavort and strut, showing off their beautiful courtship plumage. Until the summer molt, the males are dressed in gaudy colors that far outdo the drab coloring of the hens. If it weren't for the serious business at hand, the wildly bobbing and weaving drakes would be comical, but the battles between the rival drakes are real and heated. Drakes protect their hens with single-minded intensity.

Male rivalries are commonplace until the breeding pairs are formed and territories established. Nesting areas are jealously guarded but the ever-vigilant breeders are sometimes outsmarted by predators such as the minks and magpies that destroy the eggs. Most dabblers lay between 6 and 12 eggs but fewer than half the eggs hatch.

Summer is an active time for waterfowl, that being when the birds hatch and raise their broods and teach them the skills that mean the difference between life and death in the wild. Both drake and hen

41

A carton is a good substitute for a doll buggy.

share in the nest building and in rearing the young.

When the dabblers (also called puddle ducks) want to fly, they leap from the surface of the water and are instantly airborne, while the divers must run along the surface of the water to get into the air. During the summer molt, when the birds replace their water-repellent feathers, ducks and geese are unable to fly. The antics of temporarily grounded birds attempting to fly are something to see; they run the entire length of the lake, only to finally crash headlong into the water as they fail to get into the air.

In the fall many different types of waterfowl pass over us on their way south, but only a fraction of the migrating birds stop at the lake. Huge flocks of sandhill cranes are among those that fly over but never land. Small groups of snow geese and white-fronted geese are occasional visitors early in the year, but only a bird or two of each kind visit in the autumn. Rarely do the snows visit the lake but, when they do, their distinctive black wing tips and relatively small size easily distinguish them from the all-white swans. Shovelers and dabbling ducks, with beautiful brown-and-white breeding plumage, are also visitors but they never come in large numbers.

Autumn that year was an especially cold one in the Alaska Range and the early cold ushered in a long winter of

42

heavy snow. Many flights of waterfowl simply bypassed Loon Lake, which had frozen early. Those that did stop stood on the ice and looked somewhat bewildered, soon leaving the unfriendly environment. The last to leave were the hardy mallards, and only because of their continual swimming had a small portion of the lake been kept from freezing. When they left, the lake quickly froze over completely. Still, for some time after, flocks of northern birds would sweep in, stay for a few minutes, and then, with wild cries, beat their powerful wings and flee to the south. Other flocks would merely circle the lake and continue on.

There is something about the cries of migrating birds that arouses undefinable feelings. Under a leaden sky at the end of an Alaskan summer, to hear the wild call of a Canada goose is a stirring experience. Whether something in the very core of the listener longs for the freedom the bird seems to be expressing, I cannot say, but the sound is a compelling one. The cry of a loon on a frosty morning is eerie; the howl of a wolf on a clear winter night is haunting. But the emotions they arouse can't compare to those that come when migrating geese fly overhead. An animal excitement, a sense of joy: something of each of these rises within me when I hear the wild geese. To us, the cries of the big Canada honkers are, more than any others, the true sounds of the wilderness.

7
First Winter on Loon Lake

*I*n the first year we wintered there, Loon Lake was frozen solid by early October. Snow came on October 5 with a storm that lasted for five days. That first snowfall presaged many snows to come; by January the ground was covered with over 50 inches of snowpack.

Finally we had succeeded in severing the bonds of civilization and faced our first winter in the bush. Our daily routine was simple and, thanks to the solidly built cabin, comfortable. I usually would arise first, build a fire in the heat stove and put a pot of water on. Then I would go outside to bring in an armload of kindling. The cabin warmed quickly and by the time I had a small fire crackling in the cook-stove, Gretchen would be up, dressed and ready to make breakfast.

We were surprised to learn how simple life could be. Chores were minimal. The major weekly chores were splitting fire-wood and hauling water from a hole cut in the ice of the lake. Washing clothes was our biggest headache, and the amount of work that laundry made for Gretchen was amazing. Washing takes a lot of water, which has to be hauled, and a lot of elbow grease. We never really have solved that problem satisfactorily.

Our day ended about 10 p.m. Mary Anne would have been in bed for an hour or so before I finally put my paper, pen and books away and extinguished the gasoline lantern. Each night we let the stove die out and no matter how cold it got outside, the cabin remained warm.

Our daily activities varied. If not involved in chores, I would be out wandering through the woods photographing and studying the world around us. Some days I took my old single-shot shotgun down from its pegs and hunted for a grouse or hare for dinner. I also spent a minimum of three hours a day writing, doing correspondence and reading. That first winter I also cut spruce timber off our land for a workshop I planned to build and kept busy sledding and peeling building logs.

We had brought a treadle sewing machine out to the lake with us, and the New Cottage really got a workout that first winter as Gretchen kept busy making new clothes and mending others. We had purchased the 40-year-old machine at a Fairbanks rummage sale and Gretchen carefully reworked and repaired it. She also had the usual domestic chores, such as cooking and looking after Mary Anne, to keep her occupied. How she finds time to do all the things she does is beyond me. In addition to other activities, she usually sketches every day and paints wildlife and scenery.

A multiband portable radio was our daily link with the world. Usually we could pick up most Anchorage and Fairbanks stations, Radio Moscow, the Voice of America and a shrill-voiced

A beard looks warm, but it sure freezes fast. In really cold weather, a beard speeds up frostbite.

woman who seemed to run Radio China single-handed.

Our life may have been simple and uncluttered but we never lacked for worthwhile things to do. At times we did get cabin fever and got on each others' nerves, usually when heavy snowfalls kept us indoors, but these times were rare. Our first winter in the bush was a satisfying and happy one.

In late December that year, a yearling moose took up residence in the forest about 300 yards from our cabin. The

*A heavy snowfall like this one makes us realize how cozy
the cabin is and how self-sufficient our life.*

snow was deep and foraging was difficult for the young moose. Most of the time the calf wandered up and down our trail to take advantage of the firm footing. Eventually the browse along the trail and its immediate vicinity was used up and the moose was forced to flounder through the deep snow to feed. The animal struggled from tree to tree and found that under the widespread spruce limbs there was little snow and feed was exposed.

Every once in a while I would carry Mary Anne on my shoulders to look for the moose and see how it was doing. On snowshoes I could move easily through the deep snow. Once we encountered the yearling on the trail and, with ears laid back and hackles up, she challenged our right to the path. We hastily abandoned the route to her. Even though the young moose was handicapped by the heavy snow, she appeared to be wintering satisfactorily and looked healthy. We often wondered what had happened to the mother, since most animals that age are still with a cow.

One clear night toward the end of February, we heard the long wavering

46

howl of wolves. Although it came from far away, the sound carried clearly across the frozen forest. Wolves are not numerous in our area; these were the first that winter. The next day I snowshoed up the inlet stream to hunt ptarmigan. Two miles above the lake I found the fresh tracks of two wolves, undoubtedly the ones that had been howling the night before.

A few days later we found signs of the wolves again, this time close to home; when I went outside one morning to get

A ptarmigan in winter. Plumage will change to brown in the summer.

some kindling I saw the unmistakable tracks on the packed snow. Two wolves had come within 15 yards of the cabin. Later that day I discovered that the wolves had killed the moose.

The yearling had been feeding along the packed trail when the wolves had found her. From the tracks in the snow, I could see how the moose had turned to fight, but the wolves had maneuvered the moose off the trail into the deep snow where she floundered. Snow around the remains of the moose was crimson with blood, and patches of hair and hide lay scattered about the kill. Close by, several beds where the wolves had rested after feeding showed plainly in the snow. A large area around the carcass had been packed down by the predators and their droppings littered the area.

The evidence of the moose's demise was graphically recorded in the snow. Once the animal floundered, the wolves closed in, attacking from the rear. Working their way across the moose's midsection, the wolves tore the animal apart while it was still alive. The wolves had left some time before I found the carcass and had eaten only part of the hindquarters and the guts. The front half of the animal, except for minor slashes, was intact. The moose had struggled successfully against hunger all winter and it seemed to us that she deserved a better fate than she received.

The snows of winter, like the pages of a good book, each have something different to tell. The fate of our moose was one such story.

The white landscapes record the activities of all the animals that call the forest home. Ptarmigan make easily recognized strings of oval prints as they wander from bush to bush. Mink tracks suggest curiosity as they string across the snow. The ribbonlike trail of an otter records the animal's sense of play as it runs and slides. Such a trail starts mysteriously from a tiny hole and loops from bush to hummock, then disappears under the snow until whim brings the otter back to the surface for more wintertime fun.

One time I saw the trail of an otter on the ice and started past with only a fleeting glance until I realized there was something strange about the tracks and stopped to investigate. Over the trail left by the sliding otter, the big prints of a lynx showed plainly. The lynx had followed the otter for some distance. I tracked the pair and found where they met. The lynx had attacked the otter, but the tough weasel had proved too much of an adversary for the lynx; only a minor skirmish had taken place. The tracks went their separate ways after the encounter.

Tracks of the squirrel go straight from one tree to another. The squirrel, in terror, moves in leaps, only briefly daring to leave the refuge of the treetops. Its hunter, the marten, leaves tracks that lead helter-skelter as the marten investigates every nook where a squirrel might be hiding. Occasionally, tracks of the shrew appear on the snow at the base of a protruding twig, looking so fragile that they might have been made by a leaf being blown capriciously along the soft snow.

The winter cover records tragedies on several scales. One time I saw in the new-fallen snow a place where the tracks of a snowshoe hare seemed to disappear. A few feet away churned and bloody snow revealed the wing marks of a great horned owl and the spot where it had killed the hare. Another time I followed a grizzly bear's trail through the snow. Twice I found places where the bear had made leaps of six feet or more and each time a small red splotch in the snow revealed that the grizzly—the biggest predator in North America—was effortlessly catching snowshoe hares.

There are different kinds of snow. New-fallen snow yields almost silently underfoot. Midwinter snow is dry, and squeaks and crunches as one walks through it, while spring snow is tired and crackles as the crust resists, then breaks. Wind-driven snow is riffled like lace or like the whitecaps of the sea, and it sparkles with flashes of blue, yellow, orange and green.

Soft wet snow clings to tree limbs, but close examination reveals tiny fingers of ice under the snow holding the twigs and branches much like grasping birds' feet. When the load becomes too heavy, or a breeze sways the branches, bushels of snow cascade downward and the tree stands conspicuous and naked next to its whitened neighbors.

Our cabin sits in the snow like an oversize malemute braced against the wind. Because it is built of logs, the house seems almost a natural part of the scene. Beside the cabin an ancient birch tree, many of its branches snapped off by high winds, stands as a lone sentinel. Behind the cabin are tall, stout trees decked in lichens; with snow on their limbs, they remind me of gentlemen swathed in ermine. A lacy growth resembling Spanish moss, draped in loops from some of the spruce, is whipped by the wind into intricate, snowy, cats' cradles.

The winter forest is beautiful and wondrous but it takes only the bone-chilling days and howling, biting winds to remind us that winter is essentially a time of struggle in the northland. Primitive peoples often reckoned years in terms of winters. Many northern people, even though civilized far beyond that primitive stage, find themselves measuring their lives in winters, too, for the harsh season leaves its mark as surely as notches cut in an ancient calendar.

8
Hauling in Supplies

Our first winter at Loon Lake was a busy one and, like most people who move into a new home, we had a lot of work to do to make ourselves comfortable. It always amazes me when I realize how much a family can accumulate. A mound of our clothing, books, housewares and bric-a-brac was piled up in a friend's garage in Fairbanks awaiting transfer to our new home. Moving all of that to the lake seemed like a monumental task, one that would require some form of transportation other than our usual backpack.

A snow machine could not only offer a suitable method of carrying our belongings to the cabin but could also provide winter transportation to and from the lake on a permanent basis. When I first saw Loon Lake, the nearest road ended at Cache Creek, but by the time we had our cabin built, the state had constructed the George Parks Highway between Anchorage and Fairbanks. We had already demonstrated that we could travel overland from the new highway by snow machine, but we had mixed feelings about owning a machine ourselves.

I have never really liked snow machines because they seemed to me to be noisy undependable gas hogs—expensive ones, too. I have used several different machines over the years and they all seemed to be alike—unreliable. We hesitantly looked around at the different makes and models, but in the end it was a friend who sold us on the kind of machine that we finally bought. Our friend, a trapper, swore that the machine he recommended was "all figured out" and really trustworthy. Although the machine is far noisier than we would like, it has proved to be just as dependable as he said it would be.

We also bought a folding sled to tow behind the machine, and during that first winter we used our new acquisitions to make several trips to Fairbanks to pick up loads of gear and bring them back to the lake.

Our winter trail is normally good, but that winter heavy snowfall and wind combined to obliterate the trail regularly. Hauling a load of gear or a sledload of wife and child proved to be either an easy task or a practically impossible one, depending on the weather. If the trail was covered over, the journey became arduous. The little machine could not haul a heavy load through unbroken snow, and under such conditions I would have to take the machine ahead, unloaded, pack down a good trail, then go back to pick up the gear or passengers. On a cold day this procedure was time-consuming, unpleasant and not without hazard. On a packed trail the trip was not bad, and was sometimes even pleasant, but whatever the conditions, we made it a point to travel light when all three of us

went to town. Snowshoes were an essential safety item for every trip, as were matches in a waterproof container.

On very cold days, when the temperature was minus 20 degrees or colder, I avoided using the machine because of the risk of frostbite. Wind generated by a moving machine quickly lowers the chill factor to dangerous levels. On occasion, however, I had no choice but to take the machine out regardless of weather.

One day in early February we ran out of lantern gas and I had to make a trip to Talkeetna for more. The temperature was minus 10 degrees when I left. On the flats above the cabin the wind had obliterated the trail and was whisking along at about 10 mph. The wind-chill factor was near minus 30 degrees, and the journey out to the highway was long and cold even though I had the wind at my back most of the way.

I had dressed for the weather but, despite the heavy insulated snowpants, parka, arctic mittens and face mask, I had to stop several times to warm up. The combination of the low temperature and the wind was just too much for an extended period. My eyes watered almost the whole time and my lashes were constantly freezing together.

Late that day I started home. The temperature had dropped to minus 15 and, for most of the way back, I was forced to head almost directly into the

*A snow machine with sled attached is essential for getting
supplies and equipment to the cabin.*

wind, which blew steadily out of the north. My face mask became covered with ice, and several times I had to take it off to beat the frost from it. At such times the wind-driven snow stung like buckshot when it struck my exposed flesh.

Barely a mile from the lake, on the flats above it, the wind was kicking up a ground blizzard and I lost the trail. Even without the trail, I knew which way to go and I headed toward the cabin, but the swirling snow made the going difficult and slow. A half-mile from the shelter of the timber above the lake, near-disaster struck.

I was going down a slight incline when the machine suddenly plunged into overflow—water that had come up over the ice but had not been visible because of a covering of snow. The machine ground to a halt in water that was eight inches deep. I had to get the machine out of the icy water before it froze in, and that meant getting myself dangerously wet.

I had no choice but to step into the flowing water. My feet were already numb from the ride, but I felt the jolt of cold as water filled my boots. I worked quickly, pushing and lifting the machine toward solid snow. The engine idled smoothly but the track barely turned because it was starting to freeze into place. My mittens were soaked and I lost feeling in my hands. Finally I managed to get the machine out of the overflow and onto solid snow, and as I pounded ice from the track with my clenched fist the blowing snow whizzed by me with increased force. Once clear of ice, the machine moved well and I quickly made the shelter of the trees and was soon home. I rushed into the cabin and stripped off my frozen boots and mittens. My feet and toes were a pale white and completely numb, but after 10 minutes by the roaring stove, I began to feel the numbness slowly leaving my feet. The thawing was painful, but I was lucky to escape with only minor frostbite.

Without a doubt, getting in and out of the bush for supplies and groceries is our single biggest headache. Simple tasks become complicated and frustrating when we do not have all the necessary items on hand for a project. One time I was in the middle of building a tool cabinet when I ran out of nails. A 15-minute project took an hour as I hunted high and low for more nails. Shortages that are trivial in the city become major roadblocks in the bush. No matter how carefully we try to plan ahead and prepare for such contingencies, we always seem to end up with a long list of minor items to purchase in town. Once Gretchen started to make cinnamon rolls. I had carefully split very small kindling for the stove so that she could have easily controlled heat. She mixed all the ingredients and then reached for the cinnamon. The spice can was empty, and we ate plain rolls. Such is life in the bush, I thought.

As the winter grew old, the number of sunny days increased and temperatures began to moderate. That winter we recorded a low of minus 30 as our coldest day, but when spring approached, the daily highs went above the freezing level. A hard crust began to form on the surface of the snowpack and in the early daylight hours the snow was hard and crusty enough to support the machine off the trail. In fact, the crust was so hard that the machine did not even leave a track. By late afternoon however, the snow became soft and the going impossible for off-trail maneuvering. I decided that by working in the early morning I could take

Building materials stacked up prior to hauling.

advantage of the crust and use the snowmobile to drag in logs for the workshop I was planning to build.

One morning I cut and limbed some spruce trees and in the afternoon, when the snow was soft, I packed down a solid trail with snowshoes. The first thing the next morning I ran the machine over the new trail and up to the first log. After I turned the machine around, I lifted one end of the log onto the rear of the machine and fastened it there. I gave the machine a little gas and it moved easily with the log in tow. In five days I had 18 25-foot logs piled near the proposed building site. The workshop would be 10 by 12 feet, and I planned on cutting the logs in half to get the necessary number of rounds. I was glad I had done the job when I did; two days after I finished, the temperatures climbed to the low 40s and the packed trails became lost in the slush. Using the snow machine to move logs saved a lot of work—it sure beat a come-along and a Handyman Jack!

As the cold weather waned and spring came on, the skies that had spread snow most of the winter cleared and we enjoyed day after day of dazzlingly beautiful weather. McKinley and Foraker stood cleanly against the skyline, their summits seldom hidden by clouds. Early most mornings, the peaks would be bathed in a beautiful crimson alpenglow. The rosy color would come slowly at first as the sun struggled above the horizon, but as the light grew stronger the scarlet slopes seemed to throb with life. When the light grew brighter, the red would fade and the mountains turn white. In the early light of day, the outlines of minor peaks, ridges and cliffs stood out in sharp relief. On occasion, after a blazing-white winter day, the high peaks would withdraw behind a swirl of small clouds. But by the next morning, the shroud would have dissipated and the peaks would again stand in the glow of dawn.

We had seldom enjoyed such a glorious prelude to spring. The temperatures varied little with the daily low near 20 degrees. The woods were alive with redpolls, chickadees and white-crowned sparrows and we were out each day enjoying the weather and ourselves.

The weather was ideal for sledding, and Gretchen and I played like children on the slope in front of the cabin, taking turns riding with 2½-year-old Mary Anne. It was a pleasant diversion from the logging chores that kept me busy in the mornings.

On April 22, a good month before the snow finally disappeared, I was out walking through the woods with my camera. I was after some pictures of spruce hens and walked past a trail in the snow before I realized what I had seen. It was the track of a black bear—the first bruin of the spring.

*Down she goes! With all of us taking turns on an improvised sled,
our "toboggan run" is kept in good condition.*

Then, on April 25, with several feet of snow still on the ground and the lake solidly frozen, two trumpeter swans came home. I was out splitting firewood when I heard the unmistakable call of the approaching birds. At first I thought I was hearing things, but it came again. I shouted to Gretchen, who was inside baking, and rushed off to the lake. She hurried after me and together we walked to the water. Near the outlet, two trumpeter swans stood looking at us. We approached slowly and watched the swans move clumsily through the snow. We must have gotten too close to them, for suddenly they sprang into the air and with wild bugling winged away. Later that day, though, they came back and settled down in a small lead of open water at the lake's outlet.

Bear tracks and swans! Summer could not be far off. It had been a long winter, one involving a great deal of work, but it had been pleasant and satisfying. We had finally succeeded in doing what we had always wanted to do and we had enjoyed it. However, now that winter was nearly at an end, we were anxious for the thaw and the start of summer. We had a long list of chores that needed doing once the snow was gone but, despite the anticipated labor, we looked forward to walking once again through the green woods and enjoying the summer breezes.

The view from the lakeshore: Mount McKinley and its reflection in Loon Lake.

Right—A loon flexing its wings. Loons are known for their distinctive call, which has been described as a yodel, a wail or maniacal laughter.
Below, right—One of the brightest of wild flowers: the wild iris, also known as the wild flag.
Below—This porcupine is probably hoping to nibble one of my ax handles for lunch.
Opposite—Waterfowl's view of the cabin in summer.

Above—Mountains of the McKinley group in the background; Loon Lake and water lilies in the foreground. Right—Wild raspberries, either fresh or as preserves, are delicious eating.

Above—A spruce grouse hen.
Grouse, being tame, are easy to
photograph or shoot.
Left—Close-up of an inside corner of
the cabin during construction.

*Gretchen and Mary Anne
awaiting arrival of a floatplane.*

*Left—Trumpeter
swan in flight.*

*Above—Skewered with a green willow
twig, shish kebabs are a tasty
meal, whatever the combination of
vegetables and meat.*
*Left—A grizzly bear: an occasional
visitor in the Loon Lake area.*

63

Right—Currants, which are tart, are best used for jelly or jam although Indians once used them for wine.
Below—A bull moose's antlers are a formidable weapon against another bull in the rutting season, but by the end of November the antlers have been shed.

Left—The cabin door, with a caribou shovel as decoration. Below—Footprints of a grizzly in sand near the lake. Note indentations made by the claws at top of photo.

Above—View over the frozen lake in early spring. Right—Winter snowpack on the workshop. Roof has already been shoveled to reduce weight of the snow.

Left—Gretchen's fresh bread not only tastes good but gives a wonderful fragrance to the cabin. Below—A delighted Mary Anne with the snowshoes that Gretchen made.

Above—First stage of workshop construction: using the snow machine to haul logs to the site. Right—A snowshow hare: a good example of camouflage.

Left—Fresh snow, a plastic tarp and smooth sledding for Gretchen and Mary Anne.
Below—Finished corner of the workshop, showing Hudson Bay method of construction.

69

*One of my wintertime chores: shoveling three feet of fresh snow
off the roof of the cabin.*

Below—Mary Anne with one more form of winter transportation.
Right—Although low by some standards, our average winter temperatures make us feel as if we're living in the local Banana Belt.

Above—Food like Grandmother used to make, and probably made in an oven similar to the one she used.

71

Below—It's easy to know who your bird or animal neighbors are when there's snow on the ground. Right—Gretchen and Mary Anne during a memorable Christmas celebration.

9
Summer Projects

On May 1 the thermometer stood at 54 degrees, the highest temperature since September 27 of the previous year. Slowly the snowpack condensed and receded under dreary, cloudy skies. The snow underfoot was rotten, and walking through the woods, even on trails, was difficult. But we had business to attend to in Fairbanks and we would have to leave our cabin for a while. Early on May 3 we showshoed out to the highway.

We left home under leaden, gray skies and walked out on rotten snow. Three weeks later we returned on a clear, warm day. Except for patches of snow that persisted in the shadowy woods, winter had vanished. The ice had gone out and

waterfowl swam placidly about in the still-cold waters of the lake.

A great deal of work lay before us that summer. First I wanted to deal with a job left over from the previous year. Several big piles of brush and log trash that had accumulated during the cabin construction had to be carefully burned. I spent a week piling and burning it all. The dead branches and limbs had dried thoroughly the previous summer and burned vigorously. I had to keep the piles small, for wildfires are a very real hazard in the bush. For the same reason, the burning had to be the first item on our agenda: the trash had to be burned while the soil and undergrowth were still wet from the snow melt.

After I burned the brush, and before any new projects could be undertaken, I wanted to collect some of the firewood that had been hidden under the snow. The previous summer I had not gotten a chance to bring in all the firewood that we had cut before the snows came and covered some of it. We spent two days locating and hauling in the spruce and birch firewood, and were able to collect most of it before the summer's brush growth swallowed the scattered piles. The few days spent hauling firewood resulted in a surprisingly large pile, one that lasted us well into the following winter.

Our summer project list was headed by three important jobs: building a food cache, a workshop and a gasoline cache. I spent some time carefully preparing my tools before beginning the summer's work. Axes had to be sharpened, as did the drawknife and chain saw. I carefully checked over and cleaned my other tools, too. Gretchen wanted to put in a large vegetable garden and while I worked on my tools she began preparing the soil for planting.

Gretchen worked hard to turn the soil and cut through the sod for her garden. She dug up and cultivated two plots: one on the slope and one on the flat by our spring. One site was fairly dry and sunny while the other was shaded and moist. With high expectations she planted potatoes, carrots, peas, radishes and cabbage. As an experiment she also planted corn, wax beans, spinach, kale, comfrey, parsley, sage, thyme and mint. Some of these things were planted as a shot-in-the-dark experiment but we tried them, anyway.

After all the firewood was in and stacked, I began work on a cache. A cache is as old as the Alaskan scene itself and has proved through the years to be a useful and practical supplement to a bush cabin, providing outside storage of perishables and valuables while keeping them safe from bears and rodents. Our cache would be used for meat in winter and other food in summer. We wanted to build the cache fairly small, yet make it big enough to be practical. We settled on a size of 3 feet by 3 feet for the floor, altering the traditional design by putting in shelves and making the walls 3½ feet high—higher than on most caches with floors of that size. The finished product would be 8 feet off the ground.

Piled near the cabin was a stack of small log ends that we had accumulated during cabin construction. The dried logs peeled easily and I found that there were enough pieces for the cache itself but none long enough for the legs. I cut and peeled four 12-foot spruce poles to use as the uprights. Then I dug four holes, each 4 feet deep, creosoted the poles and stood them on end in the holes. Our cache was to be built something like those tradi-

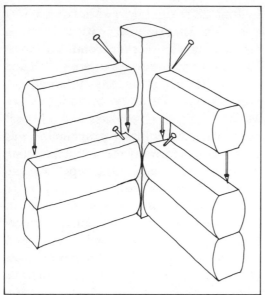

Diagram 5: *Hudson Bay Method of Log Building — Instead of being notched at the ends, logs are toenailed to uprights. Although easy to do, this method does not offer the strength and attractiveness of saddle notching.*

tionally used by trappers but, instead of notching the small wall logs of the cache, I put the logs up in the Hudson Bay method. Rather than being notched and fitted together, the wall logs are adzed flat on two sides, cut the appropriate length, and then spiked to uprights at each of the four corners (diagram 5). The simple upright construction proved to be fast and easy, and as a result I decided I would build our shop in the Hudson Bay style, too.

I spent three days assembling the cache legs and their top support and the cache itself. First I fitted a framework of four notched logs to the top of the cache legs. The legs of the cache were 5 feet apart at ground level and tapered in to 3 feet, where the framework of logs formed the base of the cache. I then used some light cable and turnbuckles to brace and strengthen the legs.

The actual construction of the cache itself took only one day. In order for the corners to have a smooth fit, the uprights were made of smoothed quartered logs. The uprights were toenailed in place with big nails (to toenail is to drive in a nail at an oblique angle). Then I measured the distance between the uprights and cut all the wall logs accordingly. Before putting up the wall logs, I nailed in some boards to serve as the floor of the cache. The walls went up fast. I would place a small log between the uprights, toenail it in place and then lay some moss along the length of the log to serve as insulation. Another log was placed over the first, toenailed to the uprights and nailed to the lower log. The process was repeated on all four sides until the walls were flush with the top of the 3½-foot uprights. When I completed the gables, the ridge-pole sat 4 feet above the floor of the cache. For the roof I used an old scrap of plywood covered with plastic, which in turn was covered with 3 inches of dirt and sod. The sod would help insulate the cache and keep the interior and its contents cool in summer. Using my chain saw, I cut out the door and used a piece of plywood decorated with dried spruce as the door itself. As a finishing touch, I flattened four gasoline cans and nailed them around the legs of the cache to keep out climbing animals.

The cache was put to use immediately as we began storing food in it as well as other items that needed to be kept cool. As a precaution in case of fire, we also stored two sleeping bags and some extra clothes in it. If we were ever burned out in the middle of the night, we would at least have some protection from the cold and have clothes to wear.

Hudson Bay corners may lack the aesthetic appeal and the strength of saddle notches, but they are a quick, easy way to build with logs. It usually takes me a day to put down two complete rounds of logs on a cabin when using saddle notches, but it takes only half the time with Hudson Bay corners.

After I built the cache, shortly before the first heavy rains of summer, we began to notice the first mosquitoes of the year. The snow melt had left the woods and swamps saturated with moisture and, as the clear skies of early spring gave way to the rainy skies of summer, the number of mosquitoes increased almost daily. The first ones showed up around June 14 and by June 28 mosquitoes swarmed about us in hordes. That summer, with continuous rain and cloudy weather, conditions were ideal for the mosquitoes to breed. Clouds of the tenacious insects followed us everywhere, constantly buzzing as we worked on our projects. A liberal application of insect repellent was imperative before anyone stepped outside the cabin but, despite the repellent, the insects still managed to bite and raise welts on all of us. They were worst on Mary Anne since she lacked the experience to protect herself, and any exposed flesh was soon covered with mosquitoes. On some cool, humid evenings, when the wind stilled and we worked outside, the bugs climbed into our ears and around our eyes, repellent having no effect.

By July 5 the number of mosquitoes began to decline to a more tolerable level. The worst part of that brief plague was that the insects were inescapable. They got into the cabin whenever the door was opened during the day and attacked us when we went to bed. Other mosquitoes flew down the stovepipe and crawled out holes in the stoves. Finally we burned mosquito-repellent coils at night in order to get a few hours of uninterrupted sleep. Often just the constant drone of the insects was enough to keep us from enjoying a peaceful night.

As the wet weather continued, our newly built cache began to tilt slightly because the soil about its legs turned to mud. I easily corrected the lean by adjusting the turnbuckles and cables that braced the legs. After the initial settling and the corresponding adjustment of the cables, we had no further trouble with the cache.

The rains continued unabated as summer blossomed about us. An entry in our diary for that period looks pretty dreary:

> June 17: Rain.
> June 18: Rain. Cloudy in p.m. Peeled
> logs for workshop.
> June 19: Rain. Porcupine on porch a.m.
> June 20: Rain.

The first flowers to bloom that summer were on the small, low-lying plants: strawberry, dewberry, blueberry, bog violet, white starflower and bog rosemary. Next came the taller plants like Labrador tea, highbush cranberry, currant, raspberry, bluebells, cow parsnip and wild geranium.

The lake was high and covered with stands of water lilies. The large yellow pond lilies had great red-tinged leaves that curved up at the edges, while the dwarf white pond lilies laid flat and supple on the water. The heavy rains that brought swarms of mosquitoes and made working outside a wet, sloppy chore also brought new life to the wilderness and gave us a bumper crop of berries.

A summer afternoon: ram's horns decorate the porch and a kitten enjoys some rare sunshine.

One morning a loud gnawing on the side of the cabin roused us from a fitful sleep. Gretchen got up to see what was making the noise and in the dim light I saw her peer out the window, grab her broom, and step outside. Almost instantly the grating stopped and a few minutes later I heard some muffled words and a heavy thumping.

"That was the biggest porcupine I ever saw," I can remember her saying as she came back into the cabin. The broom was full of quills when she put it back behind the door.

Porcupines are common around Loon Lake, and it's not unusual for one to wake us up in the morning with its gnawing. The grating can sound surprisingly loud inside the cabin when a porky is gnawing on the outside, and usually one of us has to drive the animal away before we can go back to sleep. Porcupines can be quite destructive—they'll eat anything salty and gnaw on the cabin regularly to get at the spilled dishwater on the porch or the salt in the plywood. We always hang up axes and tools after using them so that the bothersome rodents won't eat the handles to get the salt from sweaty hands.

Porkies are lumbering and slow-moving, and we can hear one coming through the brush for some distance before it arrives at the cabin. As a matter of fact, moving porcupines make as much noise as the larger black bears. Lots of times we think we hear a bear outside the cabin only to look out and see a strolling porky. A porcupine doesn't need to move quietly since nature has endowed it with a perfect coat of quills. We have noticed that porcupines don't shoot their quills, as the old wives' tales have it but, rather, deliver their quills by slapping their tails into their foes. On occasion we have heard of trappers catching foxes and coyotes with quills embedded in their mouths, and we ourselves have had the chore of removing quills from the jaws of a dog. Once with my spotting scope I saw a brown bear sow with quills on her face from below the jaw to well above the eyes.

But porcupines are not completely invulnerable. One day in early summer I was out exploring the country when I was attracted to a tree by the sounds of ravens squawking loudly. As I approached, I saw two ravens sitting in the uppermost limbs of a small spruce, alternately squawking and pecking at something hidden by the branches. As I drew nearer I saw that it was a porky with his quills up. The big birds were sitting on either side of the animal, only a few inches from the quills. The quills were raised in a defensive manner but, because of its position, with all four feet grasping the tree, the porcupine could not get the balance necessary to swat its tail at the ravens. The rodent could only cling helplessly to the tree trunk as the birds pecked with their stout beaks at its face and at flesh exposed by the raised quills. When I went back the next day to see how the porky had fared, I found it dead and partially eaten at the foot of the tree.

The rain that summer kept up constantly, with only an occasional day of partly sunny weather to break the spell. In fact, within a two-month period it cleared up enough to see the mountains only five times. Despite the heavy rains and sloppy ground, I proceeded to work on the small workshop. I had the logs to prepare and spent three days, mostly in torrential downpours, peeling and adzing them.

Our plan called for a workshop with interior dimensions of 10 by 12 feet and having two windows, one facing south and one facing west. The cabin's axis would run north and south, with the door opening to the north. The door would be built of two-by-six tongue-and-groove

Our cache, complete with ferns on the sod roof.

decking and be similar to the door of the main cabin but minus the frills. The walls were to be 6 feet high and would go up in the Hudson Bay style. Instead of two purlins and one ridgepole to support the roof, our plan called for just one oversize ridgepole.

During a break in the almost continuous rain, I dug the six 4-foot-deep holes for the shop's support posts. I then creosoted six 6-foot peeled birch posts and sank them in the holes. I leveled the tops of the posts in much the same manner as I had leveled the posts used for the main cabin, using a line and a line level. Instead of the three building-support logs that we had used for the main cabin foundation, I set two heavy logs, 14 feet long and 10 feet apart, each supported by three posts, as the parallel building supports. Two hefty logs 12 feet apart and at right angles to the base logs finished the rectangular foundation of the cabin. I carefully fitted small spruce poles 2 feet apart onto the base logs to use as floor joists, each of these joists being saddle notched for a snug fit on the base logs. Then I laid a plywood floor. Besides the door and windows, the plywood floor was the only commercial material I used in the entire workshop.

After the floor was down, I cut and adzed the four corner posts and spiked them into upright positions at each corner. A fifth upright, adzed flat on two

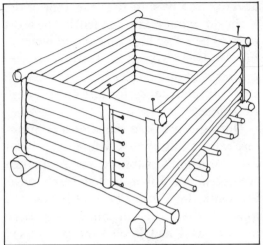

Diagram 6: *Back Wall of the Workshop — An adzed upright was placed at each corner of the building and at the door opening. Wall logs were toenailed to the uprights except for the logs ending at the door opening; those logs were spiked to the door-opening upright. A long log that would be part of the gable was spiked from one corner upright to the other and into the door-opening upright.*

sides, was placed in position on the back wall to form one side of the door opening (diagram 6). The uprights were 6 feet long and made from the hard birch instead of spruce, but the wall logs and floor joists were all cut from spruce. Spruce dries faster than wood from deciduous trees, and is lighter in weight and therefore easier to work with than other kinds of timber.

The wall logs were peeled, adzed flat on two sides and piled by the building site.

Heavy rains held up construction for a few days but when I did get busy again, the walls went up fast. First, I measured between the sets of uprights I was working with, got the measurement and cut the wall log to that length. Then I placed a layer of sphagnum moss along the top of the line that the first wall log would rest on. I lifted the log into place and toenailed it with spikes into the uprights. I placed another layer of moss on the top of the log before putting the next log down. In this manner, I put the walls up and insulated between them as I went. With the exception of the first round, each log was spiked to the one below. I realized that the logs would not settle as well as they should because of the spikes, but for a workshop the method was ideal.

Not counting delays because of rain and chain saw breakdown, and despite the mosquitoes, I had the walls of the workshop up to the 6-foot level in just four days. When the walls were as high as the top of the uprights they were fairly sturdy—with the exception of the back wall, which had the door opening in it. That wall was quite wobbly, but after I spiked a log from corner post to corner post along the top of the wall, the problem was corrected and the entire structure was sturdier. That final log was notched at the points where it was spiked to the three uprights, making a sturdy fit.

It also had a 3-inch overhang at each end to support the notched cap log on each wall.

I spent one additional day putting up the gables and readying them for the ridgepole raising. However, when we started looking through our remaining logs for one suitable for use as a ridgepole, we found that we did not have a log big enough for the purpose. So on the far side of our land, I felled a big spruce. I cut the pole the necessary 16 feet long and removed the bark with the drawknife. The spruce was straight with a spiral grain to it, an ideal combination for a ridgepole. The main problem, of course, was to move the 15-inch-diameter log to the building site and, once there, to get it up on the building.

On a warm, partly sunny day, I tackled the task of moving the ridgepole to the cabin site. I used my come-along and, by winching the heavy green spruce from tree to tree, I finally got the pole to the cabin. It took nearly three hours to move one log 250 feet.

Getting the heavy ridgepole up onto the cabin was a backbreaking chore. I built a set of skid poles and, aided by Gretchen and the hand winch, I eventually managed to get the ridgepole in place. I finished off the gables that same day, and the shop was complete except for the roof, which would be a project for later in the summer.

10
Neighborhood Bears

One rainy morning I awoke to the sound of heavy footfalls on the front porch. Sleepily I got out of bed and stepped across the cabin to the front window. I peered out just in time to look down at the head of a small and ugly black bear. He was drenched from the heavy downpour and water dripped from his scraggly coat onto the porch. Mosquitoes buzzed about his head and the area around the bear's eyes and muzzle was a mass of insects.

I rapped on the glass and the bear looked up sharply. For a moment his eyes held mine, then he swiftly stepped off the porch into the rain and sauntered toward the heavy brush. Later that morning we found that the bear had plundered the dump and had torn up a roll of toilet paper in the outhouse.

That summer, three bears came to our home often enough so that we could easily recognize them. Hardly a week went by without a visit from at least one of them. One of the regulars was the little ugly one; another regular was a big bear that we had first encountered the previous summer. Other than tearing up the dump or walking on the porch while snooping for food—which we were careful not to let them get—neither bear caused any trouble. However, that was not the case with our third regular visitor, Trouble, a medium-size black bear that seemed to live nearby.

In the early spring we had gone on an overnight trip and had come back home to find that we had had an unwelcome visitor. Because we knew a number of bears lived in the country, we always made it a practice to nail plywood shutters over the door and windows whenever we left the cabin. So, when we got home from the overnight trip, the cabin's contents were untouched. Things left outside were also more or less as we had left them, with the exception of the snow machine, which we had stored beside the cabin in canvas and plastic. A bear had come along and for no apparent reason ripped the seat into small pieces. The canvas cover was shredded into uselessness, and foam rubber was spread all over the immediate area. Furthermore, one swipe with a paw had destroyed the windshield.

I measured the tracks in the mud around the machine and estimated the troublemaker to be of medium size, perhaps a 150-pound animal. Late that day, a bear that size came to the dump to rummage around for burned leftovers. In the following days we came to recognize that particular bear whenever it showed up in the early mornings. It had a penchant for shredding discarded items, so we kept close watch on anything stored outside.

During a midsummer trip to Anchorage to get my chain saw repaired I

Bear cubs apparently are like children: they're never too young to be inquisitive.

purchased some vinyl and foam rubber to repair the seat of the snow machine. In the time between building the cache and building the workshop, I rebuilt the seat. After some fitting and stuffing, it looked as good as new, perhaps a little lumpy but certainly sufficient for the job. After finishing, I placed a crude wooden box over the machine and felt fairly confident that the seat was protected from bears and, especially, from one bear in particular.

A couple weeks later we again went out on an overnight trip and when we got back we found that the bear had been there. I was removing the shutters from the front window and door when Gretchen, grinning, came around the corner to announce that the bear had torn up the snow machine seat again.

He certainly had. Our troublemaker, or another bear with the same-size prints and technique, had torn open the covering boards and demolished the seat. Nothing was salvageable—we found pieces scattered as far as 200 yards away.

Mary Anne was jumping up and down gleefully yelling, "Bear in trouble! Bear in trouble!" and that was how Trouble got his name.

That was not the last of our problems. One fall night while I was gone the bear attacked the clothesline, tearing several sheets into pieces and stomping a full day's worth of hand-washed laundry into the mud. Now it was Gretchen's turn to be mad.

The next day she awoke to the sound of footfalls on the porch. She climbed from bed and grabbed my shotgun, which she had loaded with buckshot, and thought about bear stew. In the dim light she made out the familiar outline of Trouble. She slipped the door latch and swung the door open, but the hinge grated loudly, causing the bear to jump just as Gretchen pulled the trigger. The old shotgun, in the close confines of the cabin, was inordinately loud. When the smoke cleared away and the ringing in her ears quit, Gretchen looked for her bear. Instead of a dead bruin lying on the porch, Gretchen found only a large hole in the screen door. At least the bear got the message, because we saw no more of him that year.

A week after she shot the screen door, Gretchen had a friend staying with her while I was away. They were wakened one day by a tapping noise and discovered the largest of our bears sitting on the front porch on his haunches as a zoo bear would sit to beg for peanuts. With his nose pressed tight against the window, he tapped lightly against the glass with his paw. "He looked so funny and so sad," Gretchen told me later, "that all I could do was laugh." As soon as the bear heard sounds inside the cabin he left, not bothering anything in the area. Afterward we wondered what the friend thought about being wakened by such a large animal and seeing Gretchen do nothing but laugh.

Because of the bear activity around the cabin and because of Mary Anne's naturally curious nature, we needed a safe place to store gasoline and other flammables. We use regular gasoline for our snow machine and chain saw and have white gasoline for our lantern. We also keep a stock of kerosene for wick lamps. It would be easy for a bear to take a swipe at a gas can and split it wide open, or for Mary Anne to disobey us and play with the cans. So the summer's third building project was construction of a storage area for flammable liquids.

Our cabin is set on a slight rise and I decided to dig into the foot of the small hill to build a storage pit for the liquids. I

One of several black bears that visit the cabin.

dug straight down, making a hole 3 feet by 3 feet. Because of the slope, one side of the cut was about 5 feet high, the other about 2 feet. I used a round-nose shovel and homemade pick to move the soil, which was very rocky and difficult to dig. When I had finished excavating, I cut some log scraps into 3-foot lengths and inside the hole I formed a log box 3 feet square and 3 feet deep. I covered the top with plywood and a door and then filled in around the box and on top of it with gravel and sod. The entire box, except for the door, which was made from a heavy half-log, was solidly buried. The bunker proved to be a safe storage area for flammables, protected as fully from a bear and a child as from an accidental spark.

For someone who prefers a different style of storage, I recommend the style of a bunker built by a friend who cut the top off a 55-gallon metal drum and sank it into the ground so the drum's top was flush with the soil. He filled in around the drum with dirt and built a log door for the top. In the summer he uses the bunker as a cooler and in the winter he stores potatoes and vegetables in it, since the surrounding soil prevents them from freezing.

Either way, you've got a good bunker for keeping things safe from an inquisitive child or neighboring bears.

11

CB Communication

Mary Anne was sick. Just a few days before, on August 3, we had celebrated her third birthday, and now she was ill. One evening after dinner she seemed extra tired so we put her to bed early. We thought it unusual that she didn't fight or offer her usual variety of excuses but instead went willingly to bed. Because her skin was cool, we assumed that she was just very tired. The next morning, however, it was quite apparent that something was wrong.

The usual sounds of starting a fire and making breakfast failed to wake Mary Anne. We had breakfast just about ready when we began to wonder about our little girl. Gretchen checked and found Punkin

still asleep. One touch of her forehead revealed a high fever.

By 10 a.m. Mary Anne was still not up and, despite our efforts to rouse her, she just fought to turn over and go back to sleep. We tried once to feed her, but she only lolled in her mother's arms, too ill to eat or even to cry.

Later that day there was no apparent change in her condition, and I began to get ready to carry her out to the highway. I took the big pack down from the cache and put a blanket in it. I also filled a water jug and got some food to take along. I didn't tell Gretchen what I was going to do, but I was determined to take Mary Anne out to the highway if she hadn't improved by the middle of the next day. At the road I could catch a ride to town, where there was a doctor.

Other than a few mouthfuls of water that we forced upon her, Mary Anne had little sustenance that day. She would sleep fitfully, waken for a short time, and then go back to sleep. Her obvious distress while awake was the most frightening symptom because she didn't cry or talk but just tossed restlessly.

A few days before her birthday, some friends had come out to see us and we wondered if Punkin had caught something from one of them. We had no way of diagnosing her illness or knowing what to do other than the usual home care. Our previously happy bush home was not so happy for those hours of our daughter's first real sickness. We had no way of communicating with anyone and although we were armed with a few medical books, mostly first-aid manuals, they were of very little help. We had only our own knowledge to rely on, and the fact that we knew so little was distressing.

The evening dragged toward night and we nervously took turns checking on Punkin. Her forehead and cheeks were still hot and she slept fitfully. When we finally went to bed that night, I was still

A birthday in the bush. A party like this one was followed by illness and purchase of a CB.

planning to go to town the next day unless Mary Anne's condition improved. Dawn came slowly the next morning and Gretchen was up early to check on our daughter. Excitedly, she called to me that Mary Anne's fever was gone.

I jumped up, hurried to her side, and looked down at Mary Anne just as her eyes opened and she looked up at us. "Mom, I wanna get up," she said, struggling to sit up. The fever had broken and although Mary Anne was still sick and slept most of that day and part of the next, the worst was over. She seemed to have no problem eating and taking fluids; what's more, she was able to cry with her usual lusty voice.

Looking back on it and reading my diary notes on her illness, I sometimes think we overreacted to the situation. A child's first illness is probably as hard on the parents as it is on the child, and being alone in the bush at such a time does little for the parents' peace of mind.

As a result of Mary Anne's sickness we decided to invest immediately in some form of radio communication. Gretchen had been studying for her ham radio operator's license for some time, but she still had quite a bit of studying to do before she could take a test for the license. Not wanting to face any further emergencies without a radio, we decided to buy a citizen's band—CB—radio. The next week, with Mary Anne back to normal, we went to town and purchased a fully transistorized 23-channel mobile unit and a long-range power-beam antenna. We also bought a heavy-duty 12-volt auto battery to power the unit.

The advantages of a CB unit over a ham station were obvious. First, we could purchase the unit and use it without a special test. The applicant files a form and gets a temporary license, later receiving a permanent Class D station license. The applicant is required to purchase *Part 95, FCC Rules and Regulations, Citizens Radio Service,* which contains the Federal Communication Commission (FCC) rules governing CB radio use. A token fee is required.

Another advantage of a CB radio was the fact that the truckers who regularly travel the Parks Highway all use CB sets tuned to Channel 14. In addition, there was a local group of CB users in the Talkeetna-Cache Creek area, most of them using Channel 19. Further assistance was available from Dorothy Jones of the Talkeetna grocery store, who, we discovered, provides yeoman service in receiving and sending messages. Help now would be available either from the highway or in the general area.

When we got back to the lake I immediately set up the radio and antenna. I put the four-element long-range antenna together and attached it to the top of a 35-foot spruce pole that I had cut for the antenna mast. With the help of Gretchen and Mary Anne, I set the base of the pole in a hole I had dug by the side of the cabin and hoisted the mast into place, securing it to the house. Next we attached the antenna cable to the radio, hooked up the battery, and turned it on. Static! It worked!

After twisting and turning the antenna we tuned the radio to Channel 14, and the voice of a trucker out on the highway came booming in. Our communication problem was solved.

Channel 19 proved to be the most active channel for us and we regularly talked to stations in Talkeetna, Trapper Creek, Willow and bush units on the Kahiltna River, Trapper Lake and in the Skwentna River country. We were pleasantly surprised to learn of the extremely wide use and importance of CB radios to many bush families. It wasn't until we had had our unit hooked up and operating for some time that we found we had neighbors. Several miles to the north of us and closer to the highway, two families, the Dave Johnstons and the Rick Ernsts, maintained homes. Between 6 and 7 o'clock each night the bush people turn on their CBs and visit with each other.

12
Food That the Land Provides

Although complete living off the land is nearly impossible in present-day Alaska, the possibilities for gathering and growing the lion's share of one's own food are unlimited. But to be successful, the project requires careful planning and attention to detail. When we lived in town we supplemented our purchased groceries with wild meat, fresh fish, home-grown vegetables and berries. When we moved to the bush, we really began to appreciate the potential of those foods for some measure of self-sufficiency.

Because of state game-animal seasons and bag limits, a bush resident cannot just go out hunting and knock off a moose or caribou any time it seems convenient. Just the same, the game regulations are still quite liberal in Alaska and by using a home canner-cooker a wilderness family can easily preserve meat for use the year round.

Properly prepared big-game meat can be great eating, surpassing beef in taste. In fact, to us and many other bush families accustomed to wild meat, beef is virtually tasteless. Poorly cared-for wild meat, on the other hand, is as bad as any meat can be. Quality game meat for the table begins with proper field care.

Gretchen shoots a moose every year for our winter supply, and care of the meat begins as soon as the animal is dead. We clean and dress the moose immediately, skinning it out completely to allow rapid cooling. We believe that speedy cooling of the meat is the essential step in the preparation of quality meat. When working on a moose, we use clear plastic as a ground cover to keep the meat from getting hair on it. Inevitably, the meat does get some hair on it as it is skinned but that can be immediately scraped off.

Properly cared-for moose meat has just about the finest flavor of Alaska's game animals; only the meat of wild mountain sheep surpasses it. We quarter the meat, pack it to camp and, if it is an early-season kill, hang up the quarters and allow the meat to age. We try to utilize every pound of our yearly meat moose. Aging should take place in 40-degree weather and the meat should be protected from insects since black flies quickly locate and spoil fresh meat. Gauze game bags placed over the quarters will protect meat from flies in most cases but on occasion the tenacious insects can spoil the meat despite the gauze. There are alternative and equally effective ways to protect the meat from bugs. Our favorite method of protecting early-season meat is to rub black pepper liberally into any cuts made in the meat. Another good method is to rub fresh blood over the cuts so that a glaze will form and keep insects from laying their eggs in the openings.

The meat can be aged for one to two weeks depending on the temperature. Of course, the colder the temperature, the longer the meat can be hung safely. We never shoot a moose during the earliest part of the season because the weather is too warm and, without refrigeration, it's impossible to prevent spoilage. We try to get our moose in the late season, which normally begins November 1. The temperatures by then are low and the meat is easily frozen. And of course there is no problem with bugs.

In the late season there are two ways to care for the meat. First, the animal can be skinned out entirely, as in early season, completely butchered, and wrapped and stored before the meat freezes. Another method that is popular, but that we seldom use, is to butcher the animal into quarters and leave the hide on the large sections of meat. The quarters with the hide on are hung in a meat cache or from a meat pole. The theory is that the hide prevents moisture from being drawn out of the meat by the extreme cold. (If the moisture is drawn out of the meat, the result is similar to freezer burn.) Portions of the meat are thawed, skinned and butchered as needed.

Alaska is one vast outdoor refrigerator in winter and our cache within that refrigerator protects meat from ravens, camp robbers and other birds—although a marten once got in the cache. When the thermometer begins to rise in spring, we butcher the remaining meat into small

92

pieces and, using our 16-quart pressure cooker, we can the meat for summer use. Canned moose meat is tenderized by the canning process and is a good substitute for fresh meat during the summer.

Gretchen sometimes dries or jerks quite a bit of the meat to use for camping and hiking trips. A good-size hunk of moose meat that has been dried in the sun can be eaten as is or reconstituted with boiling water. Jerky is made by marinating thin strips of the meat in a mixture of spices and herbs. The strips are then placed in a low-temperature oven to dry. We prefer making jerky and drying the meat in the oven to the outdoor method of drying, since the oven method eliminates the problem of flies.

In terms of harvest, moose is probably Alaska's number-one meat animal, caribou being a highly favored second. One moose supplies us with a large quantity of meat all at once, whereas it would require two or possibly three caribou to provide that amount. We have found that one moose supplemented with some mountain-sheep meat lasts us nearly a full year. Although there are no sheep in our immediate vicinity, we always manage to get some sheep meat either by shooting it ourselves elsewhere or getting it from a hunter from the Lower 48 who can't use it. The variety this gives us is a real pleasure since any meat, even moose meat, can get boring when it's

eaten day after day throughout the winter.

Small game animals also are a source of fresh meat. Spruce grouse, sometimes called fool's hen or spruce chicken, is the most common small fowl around Loon Lake. This medium-size bird well deserves the nickname fool's hen; it can be easily approached as it rests on the ground or in a tree, and will usually just sit and bob its head while peering at an intruder. The male is a beautiful dusky color with a well-defined black breast.

Spruce grouse: especially good after several days of meals that have been mostly moose meat.

Gretchen, a good hunter, shoots our annual moose as well as smaller game.

Some chest feathers and side feathers are spotted with white, but generally the birds are colored evenly. A male spruce grouse, with his red eye patch swollen and his tail feathers fanned out while he struts during the spring courtship, is a sight to see. The cocks normally act as if they have no natural enemies and, while in their courtship show, are even more unwary than usual. At such times marten and other predators catch quite a few birds.

Grouse eat buds and spruce needles in winter, and a walk through heavy timber in our area usually results in an encounter with one of these birds. A southern-fried grouse dinner can break the monotony of a winter bush diet. We like to fry the birds and serve them with potatoes and rich brown gravy. Topped off with a cobbler made from preserved blueberries, the combination makes a meal that's tough to beat.

Another woods dweller we like to find for an occasional meal is the snowshoe hare. Our area is not good rabbit country, but every now and again we are able to get one for dinner. In winter it usually is easy to find the fresh tracks of a hare and hunt up their maker. Fried rabbit makes a good meal. Some bush residents have lived for part of a winter solely on hare meat but generally it is considered too lean to provide a balanced diet. Hares are subject to tularemia, a disease also known as rabbit fever. We always check for the telltale signs of the disease—spots on the liver—before eating rabbit meat.

One of the best game dinners I ever had was roast Canada goose. Instead of skinning the bird as many people do, I plucked it. After thoroughly cleaning the goose, I basted it with butter and lightly salted it inside and out. I made a stuffing of wild celery, bread crumbs and some small pieces of canned mandarin oranges, spicing it a little with a dash of blackberry brandy and a few pieces of walnut. I then stuffed the mixture into the goose, which I popped in the oven of the wood stove. After a huge pile of firewood had been consumed, the baking operation was complete and the goose was ready to eat. Served with canned yams, the goose was great. The bird was very juicy and as tender as anything I could ever imagine. The stuffing, if not the same quality, was certainly tasty. Few game meals since have been as good.

Another of our favorite dishes is shish kebab Alaskan. The food is prepared like conventional shish kebab but wild meat and home-grown vegetables are used instead of store-bought ingredients. A good green willow stick makes a first-rate skewer and adds a uniquely Alaskan touch to the whole affair.

Our first attempts at gardening at Loon Lake were a total failure. It rained, and rained, and rained some more. The gardens were flooded into a soggy mess.

At the end of the season we had only a meager handful of radishes and two small potatoes to show for the entire effort.

Because of the failure of the garden we leaned heavily on the wild foods that grow around our home to augment our purchased supplies. We have always used natural wild foods and it was easy to substitute these for what we would have gotten from the garden. Wild plants abound in the woodlands around the lake and we used many of them for salads, teas or medicinal purposes. Bog violet, watercress, fiddlehead ferns and cow parsnip grow in abundance around our home. Gretchen regularly collects and uses the leaves and shoots of these plants as cooked greens or raw for tasty salads. A salad made from bog violets and fiddlehead ferns is a real treat. Coltsfoot is another wild plant that, when cooked like spinach, tastes great and is an excellent source of vitamin A. A plant known as twisted stalks provides greens to be eaten alone or added to salads. Locally referred to as cucumber berry, watermelon berry or mandarin berry, the plant's stalks taste much like cucumber, as do its unripe berries.

Rose hips, the fruit of the wild rose, are among the most useful of all wild edibles. A fine jelly can be made from rose hips, or they can be eaten raw. A fresh juicy rose hip, minus the seeds, is not only a treat, it is also an excellent source of vitamin C. Rose hips can be cleaned of their seeds and dried. The dried fruit makes a fine candy—a little crunchy but tasty. Most berries, in fact, can be dried in the oven and used as snacks.

There are literally hundreds of useful plants growing in profusion in the Alaskan wilderness. Gretchen is an herb-tea buff and makes teas from various plants and, on occasion, even makes tea from the twigs of a birch tree. Dandelion tea is one of her favorites. For medicinal purposes, goldenrod tea is a natural diuretic, as is horsetail tea. A tea made from wild rose blossoms is a good remedy for sore throats.

Mushrooms of all shapes and sizes, some edible and some poisonous, grow in the shadowy woods around our home. One of the most edible, and the type we like the best, is the puffball. The rough-stemmed boletus is also tasty.

All kinds of wild berries grow in profusion around us, and that summer of heavy rains made for a bumper crop. Among those that we picked most often were strawberries, currants, raspberries, cloudberries, cucumber berries, dewberries, two kinds of blueberries and three kinds of cranberries, with the highbush and lowbush varieties predominating. The highbush cranberries and mountain blueberries were particularly abundant that summer, the blueberries

Patience combined with a shiny lure results in a trout dinner.

being very sweet and juicy. The cucumber berries were a special treat because they tasted almost like fresh watermelon.

As the berries ripened Gretchen used them in many recipes including cobblers, pies, turnovers, muffins and berry pancakes. Toward the end of summer she began to preserve the berries, making jams and jellies. In four days she preserved 36 pints of mixed blueberries and currants, 10 pints of cranberries and a few jars of meat sauce. The meat sauce is made by combining lowbush cranberries, onion, celery salt and pepper. With a touch of orange added, the sauce makes a spicy garnish for meat.

We have had fresh rainbow trout from the lake in both winter and summer. In winter, rainbows can be caught through the ice and although the fishing is slow, a piece of corn or meat on a hook usually will catch a fish or two if we are patient. Sometimes the cold wind and the long wait for a bite outweigh the hunger for a fish dinner. But a frying pan full of fresh trout really livens up a winter menu.

Salmon are what first brought our attention to the lake, but by the time salmon reach the headwaters they are well into their spawning cycle and are not good eating. Some of the fish are protected by law, too, and therefore cannot be considered a dependable source of protein. We do manage to catch several salmon elsewhere, though, and make good use of them. On occasion we preserve some fish for winter but mostly we enjoy them fresh.

In summary, we have found that the wilderness can provide all manner of good things to eat. Meat, greens, berries and fish can be harvested from the woodlands around our home. Delicacies like mushrooms and herbs are there for the gathering. And even though our first attempt at gardening was a failure, garden produce can be grown most years in the rich soil. Of course, there are a few items like flour and sugar that have to be purchased but, by using what nature provides, we find that those staples are surprisingly few.

To add to our self-sufficiency, we took with us to the lake a 100-pound bag of hard red winter wheat and a hand-operated grain mill. The metal mill, which resembles a small meat grinder, has two stone disks that grind whole grain into flour. The 100-pound sack lasted six months. Gretchen would usually grind the wheat about once a week and make good-tasting bread and baked goods with the flour. In winter she did the grinding in the cabin, but in summer she ground the flour outside, and it wasn't long before

Left—Gretchen usually grinds wheat every week. Below—The results.

the birds found the spilled flour and grain near the grinding platform. One morning we looked out the window and saw a flock of 11 spruce grouse pecking at the grain from the previous day. The birds, a hen with 10 half-grown chicks, stayed near the cabin for some time and would even venture onto the porch to look for food. We tried not to bother them and enjoyed having a feeling of barnyard activity.

When we first went to the lake, the cost of sugar was sky-high as the result of a shortage. Instead of buying sugar at the inflated price, we found a man who sold us a 60-pound can of raw honey at a price lower than sugar was selling for. The can of honey lasted about five months.

The list of staples that must be bought in town varies according to the tastes of the individuals purchasing the groceries. For my family, spices, sugar, molasses, margarine, dried eggs, powdered milk, coffee, black tea and fresh fruits are the items that most often appear on the grocery list. Canned goods like tomato sauce and vegetables are also on the list, but that is largely because we were unsuccessful gardeners.

Even though we need to buy groceries, we've at least had enough success in getting food from the land so we can testify that for the knowledgeable, or those willing to learn, the wilderness can provide a variety of food and a lot of it.

13
Roofing
the Workshop

With the delays caused by the almost continual heavy rains, and the time spent working on the gas cache, the completion of the workshop fell behind schedule. A good stout roof was all that was needed to finish the job but we weren't really sure what kind of roof we wanted to put on. We knew we didn't want a conventional board roof, preferring one made of natural materials from the forest. I did not want to put a full-pole roof on the workshop for the same reason that we hadn't put one on the main cabin—it would just take too many trees.

Finally we decided to put on a half-pole roof. We remembered that a friend had put a roof on his cabin by splitting poles in two and placing the flat sides down. His half-pole roof, although time-consuming to build, used only half as many poles as a regular pole roof and it looked nicer, too.

I had several dry poles already stacked by the nearly completed workshop and figured that I would need a total of 30 poles to do the job.

I spent a lot of time gathering roof poles, all of which I wanted to be at least 6 inches in diameter and 7 feet long. I picked as much dry timber as possible, to avoid later shrinkage.

Once the poles were stacked next to the cabin, I ran a chalk line the length of each pole and split the pole by carefully

Workshop ridgepole in place, ready for the roof to be put on.

following the line with the tip of the saw blade. After a pole was split, I smoothed the flat sides with the chain saw. I laid the two halves flat side up, side by side, supporting them by a log at either end, and ran the saw blade between them until their edges fitted tightly together. The rounded sides had to be down so that I could be sure the saw wasn't cutting into the flat side. (Chain saws, if they have dull or damaged chains, cannot do precision work and will sometimes track off to one side.) Log blocks on either side of the half-poles kept them from rolling while I worked the saw blade between them. The finished halves fitted together snugly.

The next step was to split another pole and repeat the procedure. I carefully cut adjoining logs to fit together just as I had the halves. Eventually I had all the poles for one side of the roof split in half, numbered in sequence, and carefully sawed so that they would lie on the roof with as few gaps as possible between them.

I put half the poles on and then proceeded to split and fit the remaining ones. It took 32 poles split in half to make

The workshop, built at a cost of less than $100.

the entire roof. Each pole was spiked at the top to the ridgepole and at the bottom to the cap log. It took five more poles than I had figured on to finish the job and a full four days of work, only one day less than the total time it had taken to construct the workshop itself. The inside appearance of the half-logs, flat side in, was pleasing and the fit tighter than would have been possible with full poles.

I covered the entire exterior of the roof with a sheet of four-mil polyethelene plastic, and over that I laid a heavy canvas tarp. The plastic and canvas

would serve through the winter as a waterproof covering until after the spring thaw; then I could gather some dry sod to cover the roof.

Including the two windows that I purchased for the shop at a cost of $22 each, my cash outlay for the workshop was $97. The only materials used in the 10-by-12-foot cabin that were not harvested from our land were the door and door-framing materials, windows and plywood floor.

Fall was slowly coming on the country and, as if to compete with the first red leaves of fall, the waterfowl seemed to be doing an extra amount of talking and flying. As the days of August drew to an end, the woods began to smell like cranberries, the delicious smell of autumn. The ferns and grasses, although still green, became brittle with age and fell to the ground instead of yielding as we walked through them.

I left Gretchen and Mary Anne at home for several weeks while I went to the distant Brooks Range to work. When I returned to Loon Lake, I found that autumn had arrived in full vigor. Few ducks were on the lake, or had been, Gretchen reported, but overhead wedges of birds winged by in their annual travels. The golden birch swayed in the gentle breezes, and looking at the leaves of the deciduous trees as they melded with the evergreens was like looking in a kaleidoscope. The cranberry bushes had turned bright red and blended with the fallen leaves and brown grass to form a wilderness bouquet. Our cabin was in the midst of the forest's splendor.

For the first time in many days the sky was clear and blue. No sky is bluer than an autumn sky arching over golden trees and streaked with mare's-tails. The thin wispy clouds rode the wild north wind, seeming to race the waterfowl south.

Once or twice in the first few days after my return home we heard the groaning call of a rutting moose. The heavy forest kept us from seeing him but we knew by the call that it was a bull.

The first time I heard the call was early one morning when there was a light frost on the ground and fingers of ice laced along the shoreline of the lake. A stout wind blew up a swirl of golden leaves as I walked toward the water to watch the feeding swans. From across the lake I heard the bull's deep guttural grunts. At first I thought I was hearing things as the wind snatched the sound away, but then it came again, much more clearly. What a wild sound! The short hairs on the nape of my neck stood on end while I listened to the receding call. Wedges of ducks passed overhead and yellow leaves zigzagged on chill gusts, combining with the call of the bull to remind me that we would soon be into our second wilderness winter.

14
Wintertime Chores

Winter came on us slowly, almost cautiously, as if it feared that its snows and cold were not equal to the task of subduing the land. The rains of summer and fall subsided, and finally the weather turned dry and cool. Ice gripped the lake gently at first, coming at night to test its strength, only to be beaten back by the sun and wind of the following day. That unsettled time between the falling of the leaves and the arrival of winter was a pleasant one, mostly because the rains had finally ceased. The skies were so clear that the only suggestion of the snows to come were distant wispy clouds strung along the mountains.

Finally, in early October, the clouds dropped the first snows of winter. The lake, mostly frozen over by then, now froze completely, the wet flakes leaving indentations in the new ice. The storm dumped 8 to 10 inches of snow in the woods but only a trace of snow lay on the solidly frozen lake and feeder streams.

Winter conquered the creeks more slowly. The few trees and bushes that dipped their limbs into the water collected silver cuffs of ice that grew as the cold water swirled by. Gradually the ice gained a foothold on the banks and rocks and grew outward. First the sluggish pools began to freeze and solidify. In the faster-moving sections of the stream, the current resisted the ice and pushed it into solid heaps along the bank. But the cold was persistent and eventually the flowing water also submitted to winter's grip.

Soon after the weather cleared, a cold snap came and the water was totally bound. Near the outlet of the lake, and in places where the current had swept the snow away, the ice froze clear as glass, while the pockmarked ice of the lake was an opaque white. Bubbles trapped in the frozen water swirled around rocks, logs and obstructions.

After that mid-October snow, the skies cleared once again and we enjoyed day after day of cloudless blue skies. In early morning and late evening, the slanting rays of the sun tinged the mountain peaks with pinks and reds. The indirect light of day accentuated the physical features of the mountains. Temperatures varied little during those glorious days of early winter, with the high each day near 10 degrees and the low at night near minus 5.

Gretchen and Mary Anne took advantage of the solid clear ice of the lake and the moderate temperatures to go ice-skating every day. Gretchen loves skating and since a heavy cover of snow usually blankets the lake in winter, she jumped at the chance to teach Mary Anne how to skate.

Mary Anne had a pair of beginner's skates but, like most children her age, had her own ideas about such things and thought it much more fun to fall down than to stand up. One of the pleasures for the two of them was to find places where the otters had been enjoying themselves, sliding and playing and leaving a distinct impression that they were having as much fun on the ice as Mary Anne and Gretchen.

By the end of October about 6 inches of ice had formed on the lake and, without a covering of insulating snow, it promised to thicken and go deeper.

While Gretchen and Mary Anne skated and enjoyed the weather, I readied things for the harsher months to come. First I gathered a good stack of firewood for the workshop and split a pile for use in the small airtight stove that I had set up there. Gretchen planned to use the shop as a laundry room and as a place to hang the laundry to dry. A good pile of firewood would be needed to keep the cabin warm enough for her to work and to dry the clothes. She also intended to grind flour there, and, since I had several shop projects of my own, between us we would need a good supply of wood.

After splitting wood for the workshop, I started on the big pile next to the main cabin and spent a couple of days stacking firewood under the cabin eaves. I split a large pile of kindling for use in the cookstove and to use for starting fires in the heat stove. I then split a large pile of spruce and birch for use as holding

Left—Getting water in the winter.
Above—Resupplying the woodpile.

wood—large pieces that are placed on the kindling. I also collected a pile of shavings to use as fire starter. First the shavings would go in the stove, then the kindling and finally the larger holding wood.

We have always made a point of leaving a good stack of kindling, holding wood and shavings in the cabin whenever we go away for any length of time. An old unwritten law of the wilderness requires that bush people leave dry firewood and food in their cabins whenever they leave. It's a good rule; lives have been saved when people lost in the bush have stumbled onto well-supplied cabins.

We also needed a hole in the lake ice from which to draw water. In summer we easily obtained water for drinking and washing from a small spring that bubbled near our cabin. We had dug out a large hole by the spring and getting a bucket of water only entailed walking a few steps. We always kept on hand a 50-gallon galvanized can full of water, but as soon as our spring froze, and before the lake ice became strong enough to walk on, keeping the barrel full was a problem. Eventually, though, I took my ice spud and ax down to the lake. Some distance from shore I chopped a rectangular hole in the ice large enough to easily accommodate the five-gallon water cans that we had made from white-gas containers. Next I fitted a piece of scrap plywood over the hole as a cover, and over that I piled several inches of snow that I had carried from the woods, there being very little snow on the ice. The snow insulated the hole and kept it from freezing solid. Eventually, as the temperatures dropped well below zero, we added more snow to the insulating covering and only occasionally had to chip off a thin crust of ice from the water hole. About once a week we sledded a barrelful of water from the hole up to the cabin. In summer we kept the galvanized can on the porch, but in winter we set the barrel on the kitchen floor to keep it from freezing.

I also spent some time banking a wall of snow around the base of the workshop. Since the floor was not insulated and the cabin was built off the ground, the shop needed the insulating snowpack to keep heat loss through the floor to a minimum. I packed the snow up to a point where it was a few inches higher than the floor level.

While the good weather lasted, I tried a little ice fishing. I cut a small hole in the ice and sat for several hours hoping to tempt a trout into taking my bait.

Unfortunately, though, my first ice-fishing venture of the winter was a failure. No matter how I jiggled the bait, and no matter what bait I used, the rainbows were just not interested in my offerings.

By early December we had but a few inches of snow on the lake and only about 12 inches in the sheltered woods. Clear weather predominated, but the first week of December found the mercury dipping to the minus 20s. With the sudden cold snap the frost and the lake ice thickened steadily. Winter had finally arrived. By mid-March the ice was 46 inches thick.

When the cold weather hit, it came quickly. One day the temperature was a moderate 8 degrees above zero and the next day the high stood at 18 degrees below. When the first cold snap of the year came we had no way of knowing how low the mercury would go; even though the minus-20-degree weather wasn't all that severe compared to the minus-40- and minus-50-degree weather that we had endured near Fairbanks, it nevertheless was a pleasant feeling to know we had a snug, warm cabin and a large pile of firewood, and were generally prepared for a long siege of cold.

From the standpoint of weather, our first winter at Loon Lake had been a mild one, with heavy snows and moderate temperatures. During our second winter the temperature barely reached minus 25. Points south and north of us were reporting temperatures as much as 20 and 30 degrees colder than we were experiencing at the same time. One early January day our mercury registered 5 degrees above zero, while the radio was reporting Talkeetna at 35 degrees below. We attribute the Banana Belt temperatures of our area to the close proximity of the mountains and the continual movement of air masses past those rocky bulwarks.

With the first cold spell of winter upon us, we stayed indoors much of the time. The amount of sunlight filtering through the trees diminished as the days moved toward the winter solstice. The number of hours that we used our gasoline lantern and kerosene wick lamps increased daily. It was the darkness, not the cold, that kept us indoors for long periods of time. During those cold dark days of winter our lantern consumed about one gallon of white gasoline per week. One kerosene lamp used about one-quarter of that amount every two weeks, but provided less light than the lantern. Usually we lit the lantern or a wick lamp, sometimes both, at about 3 in the afternoon, and they burned until late.

We took advantage of the cold weather to work indoors and do many of the jobs that had been accumulating for just such weather. I worked for several days finishing the inside of the workshop, then built a heavy workbench of plywood and

poles. The workbench was high enough and strong enough to serve as a base for the manually powered grain mill and also as a place where I could sharpen axes and saws without having to bend over. Once I got the bench built I oiled the log walls and two shelves that I had made. I burned quite a stack of firewood while taking care of those simple tasks.

Besides the furnishings for the shop, I built a magazine rack, a bookcase to house our large collection of books on the outdoors and on Alaska, and a booster chair made out of a spruce stump for Mary Anne to use at mealtimes. Meanwhile, Gretchen had used the shop when she made a pair of small snowshoes for Mary Anne out of hand-carved alder and pieces of rawhide.

During the course of the summer and fall I had managed in one way or another to break the handles of three of the four axes that we had. It seemed like a good idea to replace the three handles before I got around to breaking the fourth. The axes to be repaired were a six-pound splitting maul; a short-handled double-bitted light-weight ax; and a Hudson Bay-style ax, similar to a tomahawk, with one edge for striking and one for chopping.

When we had last been in town, I had purchased several ax handles but, like most replacement handles, they failed to fit any of my ax heads. An ax handle

108

usually is made for a number of different-size heads and needs to be fitted to a specific one. I chipped the broken handle ends out of the ax eyes and used a felt pen to mark the amount of wood to be removed from each replacement handle. I used a wood rasp to shave the new handle to size. To drive a handle onto an ax head I struck the butt of the ax handle with a hammer. Finally, wedges were driven into

When I chop wood, Mary Anne, in her way, carries it to the woodpile.

each ax eye for further tightening. It is customary to make ax handles fit tight by using softwood wedges rather than ones of hardwood. Later, if the head loosens, it can be soaked in water and the wedges will tighten as the softwood absorbs the moisture. Once the handles were all in place, I heated a can of linseed oil and soaked the heads in it.

Inevitably, the long cold days of winter and the forced confinement began to tell on Mary Anne's behavior. Although she had a huge pile of toys stashed beneath her bed and strewn around the cabin, she grew restless and at times was bored and lonely. She likes the outdoors immensely and could not understand why she couldn't go out and play all day when her mother or father was outside. Her short life, until then, had been a very active one and she did not like the indoor routine. The demands she made on us for attention grew as the number of her hours indoors increased.

During the cold spell, we bundled her up every day and spent as much time outdoors with her as possible. Sometimes we would take her sledding for a short period or let her help us with the chores. Mary Anne always looked forward to these outdoor excursions but did not really understand the need to stay warm. We had to watch her carefully when she ventured outside because, like all small children, she didn't like wearing a hat or

109

mittens and was constantly trying to take part of her protective clothing off.

One day, with the thermometer registering 15 degrees below zero, Mary Anne was dressed to the hilt in snowpants, parka, hat and mittens, and was helping me as I split kindling for the wood stoves. I would chop a small pile of wood and Punkin would carry a stick or two at a time to the porch. A good supply of kindling had accumulated by my feet before I realized that Mary Anne was not at my side. I put the ax down, looked around, and saw my daughter happily sitting in the snow with one of her boots off. She was contentedly pouring snow into her discarded boot and did not appear to be at all aware of her bare foot resting in the snow. I gathered her up and took her into the cabin and put an end to her outdoor fun for the day. It would not have been long before her foot would have been frostbitten at those temperatures. If nothing else, we learned to keep an eye on Mary Anne whenever she was outdoors. She never complained of the cold, and wore so much clothing that she looked like an overstuffed penguin. Nevertheless, we soon realized that she easily became chilled, and during most cold spells we limited her outdoor activities to half-hour periods.

15

A Trip to Anchorage

Fortunately, the first cold snap of winter did not last long, only about 10 days; with its departure we finally received our first heavy snow of winter. Late one December afternoon when I went outside to put some scraps on the bird feeder, I noticed high thin clouds moving in from the west. A glance at the thermometer revealed that the mercury had climbed from a morning low of minus 12 to 1 degree above zero. A camp robber squawked at me from the roof of the cabin while the ever-present chickadees chirped from the surrounding birch trees. I hoped the birds would get a good meal while they still had the opportunity; all the indicators pointed toward snow.

An hour later the sun went down and night came swiftly. A waxing half-moon cast a pale glow through the trees, and a thousand stars sparkled in the black subarctic sky. About 10 o'clock I went outside for the last time before going to bed and checked the thermometer. The mercury registered plus 5 degrees and the stars and moon were masked by clouds.

We awoke to a snowstorm. Big flakes were falling, mantling the forest in white. During the night the temperature had risen to 20 degrees above zero, and four inches of new snow had fallen since 10 o'clock the previous night. It was snowing lightly when we awoke but the snowfall intensified as the clouds lowered and poured forth a white blanket. In a 24-

hour period we accumulated 10 inches of snow.

By the time the storm passed the ground was covered with between 16 to 18 inches of powder and we began to look forward to a really white Christmas. With the warmer weather and new snow, we quickly planned a short trip to Anchorage to buy groceries and other supplies, and to go Christmas shopping. Using the CB, we called a friend in Willow and asked him to relay a message to Anchorage advising friends that we would be coming to town in a few days and hoped to stay with them.

Before leaving, I needed to check the snow machine and get it ready for the trip to the highway. The early winter weather had been ideal for foot travel and, with insufficient snow to run the machine on, we had walked almost everywhere. Now I gave the machine a thorough inspection and replaced the plugs and filters. I was in the process of hooking up the sled when I noticed a crack in the rear track-support frame that I had overlooked the first time around. With just a little pressure, the frame bent out and promised to cause trouble if it wasn't welded soon. In fact, I was unsure of the machine's ability even to make it out to the highway, let alone pull a heavily loaded sled.

Gretchen had made several dozen Christmas gifts for friends and relatives and we had to take those to town to mail to the Lower 48. I was convinced that the presents combined with the weight of Gretchen and Mary Anne would be too much for the broken frame, so we got on the CB and called a Talkeetna air-taxi service, arranging to have Gretchen and Mary Anne and the mound of presents picked up. Our old truck was parked in Talkeetna, and use of the air taxi would not only help us avoid overloading the snow machine but would mean Gretchen could conveniently bring the pickup around to the trailhead and get me. With a minimum load, the machine might make the trip in one piece.

In the two days preceding our departure, the skies cleared and the temperature once again plummeted. The morning we were scheduled to leave, the radio reported 35-below weather in Talkeetna. Despite the cold, Ken Holland showed up on time in his red Super Cub. Shivering in his down coat, he reported that it had been 40 below at his house and he had spent two hours preheating and battling his plane to get it started. Once his passengers and freight were wedged inside, Ken hand-propped his plane, took off, and headed for Talkeetna.

Before I left for the highway, I got out my ever-faithful come-along to help me reinforce the cracked frame with some cable. Then I started the machine and with crossed fingers was on my way. The trail had not yet been used and the snow was unbroken, making for slow going. Despite the fact that I was dressed in what seemed to be all the clothes I owned, I was still cold. The chill factor created by the wind of the moving machine reduced the temperature to the minus 40s. The face mask I was wearing became a mass of frost as my breath condensed and froze. The wind drove at my eyes and they watered freely, that moisture also freezing on my mask. My hands and fingers were constantly going numb and I was forced to stop often and warm them next to the engine. It took more time than usual to get out to the highway because of the frequent stops. The machine stayed together but I doubt that it would have with any added weight.

I ran the machine down to Cache Creek Lodge and waited for Gretchen over coffee. When she arrived about a half-hour later, we loaded the machine onto the pickup and were on our way to Anchorage. At first there was little traffic, but by the time we got into Anchorage, the highway was jammed and we were wishing we were back home.

The major disadvantage of living in a remote area is the unavoidable trips into town to purchase supplies. After the peace and tranquility of the woods, the hustle of a city, even a little one, has a way of quickly fraying nerves and shortening tempers. The stores of Anchorage seemed

The snow machine: it solves or creates problems.

packed with shoppers and to us resembled madhouses as masses of people hurried about on their Christmas errands.

However, we survived. We got caught up on our friends and Mary Anne's, mailed our gifts, and purchased our groceries and Christmas packages. And the snow machine was back in serviceable condition.

But when we got to the trailhead, the wind was kicking up a blizzard and I wondered about the ride back to the cabin with Gretchen, Mary Anne and a heavily loaded sled. Once I had a trail broken I knew that we would have no trouble, but the trail was unbroken, so I left Gretchen and Mary Anne at the road while I ran the trail in some distance to pack it down.

I drove about halfway to the cabin and then backtracked to the highway. The first run in was difficult going because of poor visibility and because I had to find the trail, but the ride out on the packed trail was no problem.

Once back at the highway I hooked the heavily laden sled to the machine and placed Mary Anne on the front of the snow-machine seat, where she would ride on the trip home. Gretchen rode the sled runners and was ready to jump off if the machine started to bog down on the hills.

Despite the swirling snow, the trail to the halfway point was uneventful and easy. The snow wasn't falling hard enough to obliterate the trail and the temperature was relatively warm, nearly 22 degrees. I stopped the machine where I had turned around earlier and unhooked the sled. I left Mary Anne with Gretchen while I took the machine on ahead to break trail the rest of the way to the cabin. On the hill just above the cabin I turned around and retraced my route back to my waiting family.

Halfway back, the snow quit falling, vastly improving visibility. I made it back to Mary Anne and Gretchen without incident and, after a few moments, with the sled once again hooked to the machine, we continued on our journey home. About a half-mile from the cabin, near the spot where I had fallen into overflow the winter before, the trail crossed a small lake. I was following my previous route across the lake when the packed trail suddenly gave way and the

machine, sled and passengers plunged into about 12 inches of ice-cold water.

Instinctively I gunned the engine in an attempt to try to pull us out of the overflow, but I only succeeded in spinning the track and throwing icy water all over the sled and Gretchen. Mary Anne sat on the seat looking surprised and as the engine dropped to idle, she kept saying, "Let's go! Let's go! Make the machine go!" I merely grunted something to her about the snow machine not being able to swim too good, and then forced myself to step off the machine and into the water. The quick rush of cold into my boots was a shock but I went to work to get us out.

Gretchen got off the sled and sloshed around the machine to solid snow on the trail 15 yards ahead of us. I carried Mary Anne to her. With the two of them on the solid snow, I slopped back to the machine and unhitched the sled. Some of the slush thrown onto the sled was freezing already, and it was just a matter of time before the track would be too frozen to turn at all.

I started the machine and lifted and pulled it up onto the unbroken snow covering. Standing in the overflow next to the machine, I gunned the engine and pushed as hard as I could. A stream of slush shot rearward as the track jumped forward. I was able to move the machine a few yards before it sank again. Once more I got the machine moving and managed to get it up onto the packed trail.

Gretchen and Mary Anne immediately flopped down on the seat to watch and encourage as I fought the sled to the trail. I tried to pull the loaded sled toward them but the slush had weighted it down too much, so I was forced to offload all of the gear and carry it to the machine. Once the sled was empty, I lifted it fully out of the overflow and carried it to the trail by the machine.

My feet were getting cold and so were Gretchen's since she too had had to step into the water. Quickly we reloaded the sled and headed for home. The remaining run to the cabin only took us a short time and we made it home just at dark without further incident. I was becoming skilled at coping with overflow, but that was one aspect of bush life that I did not want to become too familiar with.

The next day I went back out to the highway to move our pickup to a friend's place and bring in a sledload of presents and supplies that we had cached by the trail. I rerouted the trail around the overflow and made the round trip without the slightest delay. It was snowing again by the time I got back home and had the presents and gear unloaded and into the house. Christmas was just six days away and now—in spite of the crack (now repaired) in the snow machine, the frustrations of Anchorage, and the problem of overflow—we were just about ready for the holiday.

16
Home Again

For the next two days it snowed hard but on the third day, just three days before Christmas, it cleared and we awoke to a sparkling winter's day. I was the first person outside that morning and was sweeping the snow off the porch when I spied fresh marten tracks by the woodpile. Earlier in the winter we had had an ermine living under the cabin but this was the first sign of a marten coming that close. His easily identified tracks led from the woodpile and under the cabin. After a search, I found more tracks on the far side of the cabin leading off into the trees.

After every snowstorm that winter, we found animal tracks in many different places, but only twice were they as close to the cabin as the marten had come. Otter, mink and marten tracks were the ones we most commonly encountered. As the winter wore on we noticed an increase in the signs of fur-bearers around our home compared to what we had seen during our first winter. The fur animals were obviously making a comeback from a low population point. Whether the low was due to overtrapping at some previous time or to a natural cycle, we had no way of knowing.

Along the waterways and on the lakes in our country, we had found many old, unoccupied beaver houses and many broken dams. We saw some signs of fur-bearers but there appeared to be fewer

Animal tracks near the cabin: at left, otter tracks; at right, lynx tracks.

animals than the country looked capable of supporting. In our ramblings about the area we had located several dilapidated old trappers' cabins and had even found some very old traps hung in trees. What with the empty beaver houses and the uncared-for dams, it appeared that early overtrapping may have accounted at least for the decline of the beaver population in the area.

During our second summer at Loon Lake we had found two new beaver houses on the drainage above the lake and even a new lodge on the lake itself. Clearly the beavers were making a comeback along with other fur animals.

Our second winter at Loon Lake was spent in exploration of the surrounding country and we discovered that a professional beaver trapper had long been working the drainages to the north of us. We found that he was extremely careful to farm his country rather than overtrap it, his practice being to take only one or two beavers from each lodge. Furthermore, he always set his traps well away from the lodge so that the beavers he did harvest were adults, since kits seldom venture any distance from the lodge. His wise management and self-restraint allowed the beavers to increase in number and also let them expand their range despite his harvest. He was truly a wise trapper.

Whenever out tramping in the waterways or woods, we were always delighted to find otter tracks. Those big weasels seemed to move across the snow with the least difficulty of any of the fur-bearers. They have the most remarkable manner of locomotion on snow, hopping a few steps, then sliding along for some distance on their bellies. On solid snow or ice, the otters, we found, rarely ran more than a few feet without sliding, and their distinctive tracks were easy to identify.

I once measured the tracks and slide marks of a traveling otter. Over a distance of 30 feet the otter had taken 3 steps, slid along the snow on its belly for 7 feet, hopped 4 more steps, and then slid along for 6 feet more before repeating the entire

Right—Mink tracks cross an otter slide.
Below—One of the abandoned trappers' cabins in our area.

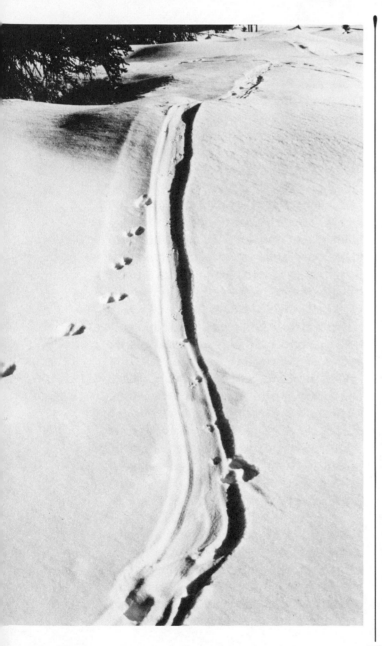

procedure. That exuberant pace was continued the entire length of the quarter-mile-long lake. For comparison, I once measured the tracks of a coyote over a similar span of hard snow. The coyote, roughly the same weight as the otter, had taken nearly 50 paces to cover the distance that the otter had covered with just 11 steps interspersed with sliding. If I had my choice, I would prefer to travel like the otter rather than the coyote.

When following otter trails, we sometimes found places where the animal would travel along the surface of the snow, then burrow under it, a tiny hole marking the end of the visible trail. Sometimes we found that the animal had gone under the snow, tunneled below the crust, and resurfaced a few feet away to continue its journey. On several occasions when we examined holes on waterways, we found where the otter had run along the surface and then had suddenly burrowed into the snow directly into the flowing water of the stream below. Somehow, possibly by smell, the otter had sensed open water below the crust and had tunneled unhesitantly to the flowing creek.

An important part of our winter explorations, not to mention trips with the snow machine, was on snowshoes. Without snowshoes, moving through deep snow is at best strenuous, and at times, like the previous winter, next to

119

Me with essentials of the bush: webs and ax.

impossible. My snowshoes were always lashed to the sled when I took the machine out to the highway so I could finish the trip on foot if the machine broke down.

Good-quality snowshoes will last a lifetime if cared for properly and will withstand very heavy use. However, finding snowshoes of good quality is not an easy task. The present market is glutted with cheap, low-quality snowshoes. One or two of the old established manufacturers of snowshoes are still producing good webs—snowshoes—but even these are not as good as the early-day models; mass marketing and mass production seem to have had an unfortunate effect on quality.

We own two styles of snowshoes: trail shoes and bear paws, one pair of each. Our trail shoes are 10 by 56; the bear paws, 10 by 36. The figures indicate the width and length in inches.

Our trail shoes are of the Alaskan design and are rather long and narrow, tapering to a thin heel. Some Alaskan trail shoes that I've seen are up to 68 inches long. Usually these extra-long models are custom-built by Indians or made on special order by a commercial manufacturer. In comparison to a Michigan-style snowshoe, which generally is 13 inches wide, an Alaskan trail web is rather narrow. The toes of the trail shoes tip up moderately and are excellent for packing and breaking trail.

Our trail shoes are of top quality, each one constructed of a one-piece frame that was carefully steamed and bent into the proper shape. The frame spacers are not overly thick and are made from one piece of hardwood rather than of spliced wood as seen on cheaper models. The spacers are inset into the frame and fit so snugly that no pins or bolts are needed.

Bear paws are shorter than trail shoes and rounded at both ends. The toes tip up only very slightly and are not the best for breaking trail. We use our bear paws primarily for walking packed trails since the bear paws are lighter than the trail shoes. The compactness of the bear paws makes them ideal for use with the snow machine and I lash them to the machine whenever traveling a packed trail.

There is no secret to learning to walk in snowshoes; all it takes is practice. Gretchen easily learned to use the trail shoes but still has difficulty with the bear paws because she finds them not tipped up enough at the toe to suit her gait. At first when she was learning to use the webs she made the task more difficult than it really was because she thought it took a special technique to use them. Once she got the idea of walking as normally as possible, she quickly mastered the basics of snowshoeing.

Snowshoes need special care but it is surprising how little that is. After using our snowshoes we always hang them outside the cabin. We have found that when we bring snowshoes into the cabin, the snow melts and is absorbed by the rawhide and wood, weakening the materials. Each spring, and also before the first winter use of the shoes, we paint a heavy coat of spar varnish on the wooden parts of each snowshoe and put linseed oil on the rawhide. Once it is dry, I paint the entire shoe with a thin coating of polyurethane varnish.

But snowshoe care was not on my mind during those few days before Christmas. I was thinking about finding the right tree for our wilderness celebration.

17

First Christmas in the Bush

The previous year, our first winter in the bush, we had spent Christmas with relatives. Now I was looking forward to our first Christmas in our cabin and the old-fashioned festivities we had planned.

Christmas Eve dawned bright and clear. The woods were drenched with sun and the weather seemed warmer than the thermometer reading of 10 degrees. As the sun rose through the trees, it cast long shadows and splashed the openings with its glare.

Gretchen rose early and started a fire in the cookstove in preparation for a long day of baking bread, pie and other goodies for the dinner that would highlight the next day's celebration. While she bustled about making whole-wheat pancakes for breakfast, I split a pile of kindling for the woodbox.

After breakfasting on a large stack of pancakes splashed with blueberry syrup, I put on my parka and went over to the workshop to wrap presents for Mary Anne. When the stove in the shop was glowing hot and the cabin warm, I removed several small toys and books from their containers and wrapped them in bright paper. What with all the presents Mary Anne would receive from her parents and grandparents, aunts and uncles, cousins and friends, she would indeed be busy the next morning opening the array of gifts that had been accumu-

Carrying home the spruce for our wilderness Christmas.

lating. Most of the presents had come by mail to Talkeetna, but a few had been brought from Anchorage by friends on their way to Fairbanks—I had gone out to the highway with the snow machine to pick them up.

By noon, Gretchen had progressed sufficiently with her baking to take time out to go with Punkin and me to cut a Christmas tree. Since most of the trees in the immediate vicinity were not shaped correctly for a pleasingly symmetrical Christmas tree, we planned to search some distance from the cabin, if need be, to locate the right tree. The trees near the lake were either too big or too small, or, if the correct size, poorly formed.

For several days prior to our tree-cutting expedition, I had kept an eye out for likely Christmas-tree candidates. Near the snowshoe trail that led north from the cabin, and along the main inlet stream to the lake, I had seen two trees that looked as if they might be just right. With these two spruce as our goal we headed north from the cabin, Gretchen carrying the ax while I walked behind pulling Mary Anne on the plastic saucer. We moved slowly, searching the forest for the right tree. After a pleasant walk on the hard-packed trail, we came to the two small spruce. Looking more closely, we found that one of them was too scrawny, but after digging the snow away from the second one, we found it to be perfect. The tree tapered in a symmetrical cone shape and was 4½ feet tall, just right for our small cabin. Two well-placed strokes of the ax brought the tree down and we were ready to head home.

While Gretchen carried the ax and pulled the empty sled, I carried the tree on my shoulder and held Mary Anne's hand. We walked silently, with only the saucer's scraping to disturb the stillness. As we moved along enjoying the warm day, I couldn't help but feel that the Christmas at hand was going to be one of our most memorable.

Back at the cabin, Gretchen returned to her baking. Mary Anne and I stayed outside to build a stand for the tree, and after some head-scratching we accomplished the chore with satisfactory results. Carefully, so as not to disturb the needles, we carried the tree into the house. Soon the pungent aroma of spruce filled the cabin and blended with the mouth-watering smell of freshly baked bread. After the bread had come golden brown from the oven, a pumpkin pie soon made its appearance, followed by tray after tray of cookies and cinnamon rolls.

Shortly after sundown, when dinner was over, we decorated the tree with Gretchen's handmade ornaments. The previous summer she had picked and preserved several dozen multicolored wild flowers. A few days before Christmas she had taken the dried flowers and placed them between clear sheets of adhesive paper, which she then cut into decorative shapes and sizes. Now she put the brightly colored wild-flower ornaments on strings, and we hung them on the tree. Next we popped a great batch of popcorn to string and drape as additional decoration, but the rich smell of the popped corn, mingling with the aroma of the baked goods, was hard to resist, and as much popcorn went into us as went on the tree. A hand-painted cutout of a chickadee topped the tree, and a bright red ribbon was the final trimming. To us, no tree had ever looked finer than this one.

Mary Anne's excitement grew as we began to pile the accumulated presents by the tree. Once all the gifts were there, the stack amazed us. Packages of every shape and size nearly obscured the tree. Just before bedtime, Gretchen brought out a tray of fudge and by the warm glow of a kerosene lamp we sat contentedly listening to the excited babble of our three-year-old daughter as she rattled boxes and poked at gifts. Knowing it would be folly to try to put Mary Anne to bed early on such a night, we let her stay up until 10, when we all went to bed.

Before blowing out the lamp, I stepped out to the porch for a breath of air. To the north the horizon was faintly glowing as the northern lights came out against the darkened sky. Brighter and brighter they grew until an unearthly green light shimmered and shifted in bands overhead. Soon the mountains stood out, clearly silhouetted against the brightening aurora. Swift shafts of light darted and raced across the sky in a changing array of colors. I took a deep breath of cold air, had one last look, and stepped inside. The cabin was dark and warm. The pungent aroma of spruce filled the room and I realized that it had been a long time since I had anticipated Christmas so much.

The sun rose as bright and beautiful on Christmas day as it had on the previous morning. Gretchen and I had expected Punkin to awaken us in eager anticipation of opening her presents but, to our surprise, she was still asleep by the time we were both up and stirring. As usual the cabin had cooled during the night but the hot stove soon had the house warm and smelling once again of spruce. Then Mary Anne was up, moving excitedly about and clutching a brightly wrapped present. I calmed her long enough for me to get some more wood into the cabin, and after I settled down with a cup of hot chocolate Mary Anne was permitted to start opening her gifts. Her eyes sparkled with excitement as each package was torn open, and her shouts of happiness were Christmas enough for Gretchen and me. Among all of her gifts, a hand-sewn doll made by an aunt and a female teddy bear named Theodora made by her grandmother were her favorites.

Besides the present of a happy child, Gretchen and I received gifts, too. I gave Gretchen a pair of cross-country skis and boots, and she gave me a watch. From friends and relatives Gretchen got clothes and books, while I received from three different people three shirts that were nearly alike.

After the initial excitement passed and the wrappings and trimmings had been cleared away, Gretchen made breakfast. Punkin was too excited to eat so we let her skip her meal. Breakfast was over quickly, and when the dishes had been cleared away, Gretchen produced a tray of cinnamon rolls, old-fashioned Christmas candy, and dates and walnuts sent to us from relatives in California.

The morning hours drifted by as we sat by the tree munching goodies and watching Mary Anne play with her gifts. We had tuned in an Anchorage radio station and had Christmas carols as background music. Punkin had received a small set of plastic farm animals from some relatives. The animals were a pig, a horse and a cow, but to Mary Anne the animals had to be wildlife. We spent a

Wilderness scene on December 25. Merry Christmas, Mary Anne!

considerable amount of time trying to convince her that the pig was not a bear, the cow was not a moose, and the horse was not some form of caribou. We wondered how many children her age had seen bear and moose and considered them familiar animals long before they saw domestic livestock.

At noon Gretchen busied herself at the stove to begin preparing our holiday meal. At about 3 o'clock dinner was ready and we sat down to eat. The main dish for our Christmas dinner was four roast spruce grouse served with a spicy rice dressing. Sweet potatoes, baked potatoes with sour cream, and whole kernel corn accompanied the grouse. Whole-wheat rolls made from hand-ground flour, along with sauce made from highbush cran-berries, highlighted the main dish.

The young grouse hens were cooked to a turn and no turkey ever tasted sweeter. The cranberry sauce had the tart fresh taste of wild berries, a flavor usually missing from canned sauce. The golden brown whole-wheat rolls, fresh and hot, had melting butter sliding on them. Pumpkin pie with whipped cream topped off one of the finest holiday meals that I have ever eaten.

As lethargic as bears emerging from hibernation, we sat around the rest of the afternoon enjoying full stomachs and the warm glow of a special day. As anticipated, our Christmas had indeed been a fine one. For Gretchen and me, Christmas had always meant family activities and large gatherings of relatives. Maybe the day should be a time of family harmony and sharing, but neither of us could remember a happier, more meaningful Christmas celebration.

McKinley and all the neighboring mountains grew pink with an alpenglow as the setting sun cast a fiery light on the perpetual snows. The evening breeze blew in the treetops, and redpolls and chickadees sang lullabies. Later, long after the kerosene lamp had been extinguished, I lay awake in the darkened cabin watching the firelight from the stove flickering on the floor. For Gretchen and me, that Christmas day, like nothing else before it, had turned our bush cabin into a very special home.

18

A Life Worth Working For

*I*n the interval since we moved from town to the bush, people have questioned us about such seemingly solitary living. The question asked most often is, "Why do you live out there like that?" It is a natural question and one easily asked, but not one to be so easily answered. Usually the person who asks the question goes on to say, "I could never leave the city and live out there that way." To such persons, accustomed as they are to the ease of urban life, it probably does appear that we are leading an unnecessarily rugged existence, and I doubt that we would ever be able to answer their question satisfactorily.

Usually the questioner does not know us very well and may try to answer the question by saying, "You don't like people; that's why you live out there." To that comment we can only say that nothing could be farther from the truth.

In the hustle of city life, people deal with one another only very superficially. Outside of their immediate families and friends, most people make contact with others only because of the demands of work and the exchange of necessary information and services. Indeed, in the extreme, people in the largest cities sometimes live for years next door to one another without ever meeting. I believe that for some of those city residents existence may be far lonelier than ours could ever be.

In the bush an encounter with another human being is an experience to be relished, a chance to enjoy that person on the basis of the individual's own worth. The value of a man or woman can be most appreciated when contact is infrequent but is really personal.

The bush hospitality that is so widely appreciated, allowing a stranger to be welcomed on a moment's notice, indicates the friendliness that many bush people feel. No, not all bush dwellers share that outlook and yes, some have gone to the bush to escape people, but I believe that they are in the minority. As one bush rat put it: "It's not that I don't like people; it's that I don't like masses of people."

In any case, for me it was animals, not people, that made me want to live in the bush. I have always had a strong affinity for the wilderness and its creatures, and it was a desire to be close to wildlife that led me to Loon Lake. As a photographer, writer and hunter of wildlife, and as a student of nature, I have spent most of my life learning about and observing wild creatures. My love of wild animals has made for a rewarding life, a life that has been greatly enriched by living in the bush. We are in contact with wildlife almost daily, and it is pure joy to be able to look out the cabin window and see a moose in winter or be awakened by a bear in summer. My only regret is that we could not make the move sooner.

One of the major factors contributing to our desire to live in the bush was our search for a better way of life. We wanted an alternative that would let us experience life and taste its real value.

In the city every convenience imaginable is available, making for an automatic, unrewarding life—often a dull one, too. I doubt if many city people realize how completely dependent they are upon others for the most basic elements of living. Only during power shortages, service slowdowns and other city crises do city residents begin to realize that life is not so automatic. They can only feel helpless in the face of such problems. Having once experienced such a slowdown and the attendant turmoil, I know that I certainly felt entirely too dependent upon people who, I am sure, cared little about me.

It may well be that in the present world it is impossible for a family to achieve

Young moose outside our window.

total self-sufficiency, but certainly one of our chief goals in moving to the bush was to reduce our dependence on other people for our comfort and for the essentials of life. We have succeeded to a large degree, although at times we are all too aware that outside forces are important for the continuance of our present way of living. We do have food to eat, water to drink and wood for heat and, in a large measure, we owe them and their availability to no one. Of course, an important part of our groceries is purchased, but nonetheless we could live on what is at hand if the need arose.

Most Americans have become so used to twentieth-century living that doing without conveniences, at whatever level, seems a foreign idea. During our second winter in the bush, two friends of ours, a man and his wife, came to see us, each driving a new snowmobile. They were pleased with our cabin and thought it nice but were very surprised to find that we cooked and heated solely with wood. They took it for granted that we would want to install propane lights as well as a propane stove and oven and, eventually, a gasoline-powered electric plant. At the dinner table they told us all about the different types of propane appliances, including a propane toilet, that were available for installation in cabins.

Those folks could not for even one moment conceive of anyone wanting to cook with wood when much "easier" methods were available. They never stopped to realize that propane stoves require fuel that would have to be hauled to the lake. It is just that kind of dependence that we were trying to minimize. Our snow machine, chain saw, gasoline lantern and kerosene lamps require plenty of fuel as it is, without more energy consumption and added dependence.

Our wood stove is of proved quality, a style used by countless numbers of people before the advent of gas and electricity, and it serves us well. Since Gretchen is able to cook or bake anything with it that she wishes, there is no reason to use a different kind of stove, and a more wasteful or expensive or less available form of energy, to accomplish the same results.

Before we moved to the bush, friends told us that we would spend all our time hauling and cutting firewood if we used wood to cook with. Some even suggested that for the two stoves we would use 10 or 12 cords of wood each winter. I suppose that with a poor-quality cabin that would be possible, but we total only 3 cords or less each winter for cooking and heating because we planned our cabin with wood stoves in mind.

To be honest, we must admit that at times we get tired of splitting kindling, and sometimes wish for better light than we get from a kerosene lamp. However, we feel such things rarely, for we well remember the times in Anchorage and Fairbanks when, in spite of twentieth-century conveniences, we fought battles with frozen pipes, nonfunctioning electric heaters or an automobile that wouldn't start. One short recollection of such problems quickly erases any momentary dissatisfaction with the way our present life is going. We have our moments of inconvenience, but living in the bush is as comfortable, more simple and more rewarding than it ever was in the city.

Two questions that we are commonly asked are comparatively easy to answer. They are "What do you do out there, anyway?" and "Don't you get bored?". Both questions always make us smile, if not laugh out loud. We have noted that some of the people who ask those questions are people who rely too much on television for entertainment and companionship. That glowing tube is one thing that we have never regretted leaving behind. As for having enough to do or becoming bored: we can only wish for hours enough to accomplish everything that we need or want to do.

Besides the time-consuming tasks of child care and day-to-day cooking and cleaning, Gretchen, one of those people blessed with a creative nature, spends time on crafts, painting and sketching. She starts her Christmas list in July and

Gretchen makes blueberry tarts for dessert.

spends hours handcrafting gifts for everyone on it.

As for me, the number of projects to be done around the cabin seems to grow daily. Future plans call for a sauna, guest cabin, storage shed, woodshed, root cellar and more. Daily chores and maintenance of wood and water supplies take time, also. Photography and writing consume vast amounts of time, more than I care to admit, and certainly the pursuit of those interests was reason enough to move to the bush. In the final analysis, we have

131

A reward of isolated living is the family closeness that can result.

more than enough to keep us occupied, and it makes leisure time all the more appreciated.

One winter day while I was in Anchorage on a shopping trip I went to an advertising agency to sell some wildlife photos that I had taken for use in an advertising campaign. The young executive I talked to was most pleased with my photographs and showed a great deal of interest in wildlife photography and our way of life.

"You know," he observed, "there just doesn't seem to be much land available in the bush. How does one go about living there?"

I knew that he was correct—there is very little land for development in the bush, and whatever land is available is hard to locate and even harder to acquire. We agreed that it is amazing that in a state the size of Alaska—586,000 square miles, one-fifth the size of continental United States—there should be so little land available for private ownership and development.

The Open-to-Entry Program of the State of Alaska, under which Gretchen and I purchased our property, has been closed by the state; the federal Homestead Act, through which land was once available at no cost at all, was discontinued later.

In any case, at the time I talked to the man in the advertising agency, the major obstacle to moving to the bush, assuming one wanted to obey the law and eventually acquire the land, was the difficulty of finding a place to buy or lease. I was able to point out to him that it would be relatively easy to live in the bush as a caretaker either for a cannery that is closed for the winter or for a lodge during the off season. Too, it would be possible to get permission from the owner of an old existing cabin, or of a mining camp, to fix up the place and live in it when the owner was not present—which in some cases is all the time. Indeed, we know a couple

Ice fishing: mother and daughter wait for a bite.

133

who did just that; they contacted the owner of a wilderness lodge and got permission to use one of the cabins during the winter months when the place was closed.

I answered the questions posed by the young man as best I could, but his detailed inquiry was difficult to respond to in the time I had. I explained that a person had to be willing to accept a complete alteration of life style, and in his case that would mean giving up a lucrative job, a nice house and two cars. Instead of earning a large salary he would have to be content with the smaller income that he would derive from some bush occupation like trapping or commercial fishing. Even if he was willing to make such alterations, I asked, what about his family; would they, too, be willing to make such changes?

That young executive expressed an interest in bush life that seems to be shared by an increasing number of people. Many of those seeking an alternative style of living have the romantic notion that a cabin in the Alaskan bush is the ideal place to fulfill their ambitions. For some, it is, but the Alaskan wilderness can also be extremely harsh, a land that is unforgiving of any weaknesses or failings in its inhabitants. One miscalculation can prove fatal. I feel that it is of paramount importance that people acquire the necessary skills and experience before they attempt the transition from the urban world to the wilderness world.

I am reminded of a story that a bush pilot once told me. He flew a middle-aged couple to a remote cabin on the Tanana River, where they were going to spend the winter. He later flew in a load of supplies for them just as the river was freezing up, and they scheduled a date for a pickup flight when he would return after spring breakup, eight months away. The pilot told me that he asked them if they wanted a check flight once every month or so, but the couple indicated that they were long-time Alaskan bush residents and didn't want the costly overflights. The pilot shrugged and said no more but planned on a check flight in the winter anyway.

For that couple, it was indeed fortunate that they had hired a reputable and conscientious pilot, because when he did make his unscheduled overflight, it was barely in time to save their lives. They had had a cabin fire a few nights before the pilot happened by, and they had not stored any spare clothing or food outside the cabin in case of such an eventuality. The temperature at the time of the fire had been 50 degrees below zero, and they had escaped from the cabin dressed in only light clothing. When the pilot so providentially happened by, both the husband and wife were near death and suffering from severe frostbite. Both eventually lost one or more fingers and some use of their legs, but they lived. Later it was learned that that was their first excursion into the bush and that they had drastically underestimated their food requirements. When they failed to find any game, they began to fear starvation. Indeed, when the fire struck, they were almost without food. They were very fortunate that the pilot had come when he did.

O ur bush home on the shore of Loon Lake is a reality. We earned it with hard work, what little money we had and determination to succeed. We found that building a life in the wilderness is a demanding goal, one that requires dogged determination coupled with a realistic sense of purpose. To those who would make their home in the bush, we offer the suggestion that they first gather the necessary skills and experience before embarking on such a move. In the process of acquiring those skills and knowledge, some people might learn that the Alaskan wilderness is not the place for them. Others will only be more positive regarding their goal, and for them we hope that they can pursue their goal with toughness and determination, that they too will finally succeed in making the bush their home.